DISCARD

TAKE ME HOME

TAKE ME HOME

The Rise of Country and Western Music

STEVEN D. PRICE

Praeger Publishers
New York • Washington

Published in the United States of America in 1974
by Praeger Publishers, Inc.
111 Fourth Avenue, New York, N.Y. 10003

© 1974 by Praeger Publishers, Inc.

Library of Congress Cataloging in Publication Data

Price, Steven D.
    Take me home.

    Bibliography: p.   ; discography: p.
    1. Country music—United States—History and criticism.
I. Title.
ML3561.C69P7   784   71-189922
ISBN 0-275-53610-2

Printed in the United States of America

CONTENTS

ACKNOWLEDGMENTS

To my parents for instilling in me a love of words and music. To Gladys Topkis, the founder of the feast, and to Léon King, for editorial guidance. To Lillian Burton Walker, Jan and James Talley, Larrimore Burton, Jr., and the other Nashville cats who showed a Yankee what Southern hospitality really is. To Jean Walker, who showed that one never need be hungry again. To the Monroe County Digitals—Kaps, Sachs, Bernie, and Specs. To Dr. M. Michael Cohen, for helping me through the nights. To all the country musicians, past and present, who have made their audiences feel right at home.

And to Susan Marx, whose lesson continues to be that the root of "encouragement" is "heart," to whom this book is dedicated.

INTRODUCTION

Recording studios in New York, Detroit, and Los Angeles reverberate with an air of hectic tension. Musicians arrive early to rehearse arrangements transcribed with great specificity. To add or delete even a grace note can throw a producer into a catatonic seizure—arrangers know best, and besides, time is money. Players and technicians walk in, do their job, then leave in anonymity.

But not so in Nashville—Music City, U.S.A. While singer and producer chat, accompanists (known as "sidemen") swap fishing stories and family gossip as they tune; everyone knows each other socially and professionally from working together five days a week, often at several sessions a day. So well do the men know each other's styles and favorite instrumental "licks" that producers, many of whom are good enough to sit in on sessions, leave the arranging to them. Sidemen are given lead sheets which show only the basic chord progressions. After they hear the melody once or twice, they retire to corners to devise what they are going to play. It seems as though they can read each others' minds, for even a first run-through is a polished blend. Studio time is sufficiently flexible to allow as many takes as necessary, and nothing causes anxiety. During one session the musicians stopped midway through a take. The producer poked his head out of the control booth to learn that "Pig's [the pianist's nickname] piano's stuck." There was no hassle over the delay, as someone simply went over and unstuck Pig's piano.

The product of such sessions has been called "the Nashville sound," coming in large measure from the musicians' total involvement with the spirit of their music, so much so that their instruments have become extensions of their hands and hearts. The sound as well as the setting is relaxed and unpretentious, just as country musicians have always gotten together for a bit of pickin' and singin'. Studio sidemen give the impression that they are sharing their finely honed skills with both the artists they accompany and the record audiences who will hear their music.

Country and western music has always been an important part of America's musical heritage. In the past few years, moreover, it has spread beyond this country's borders to become absorbed into the mainstream of worldwide culture: In its own right it has become increasingly popular in Britain, Germany, the Soviet Union, and Japan. Its appeal seems to be twofold. First, the words and music display a tremendous variety of moods and emotions, from romp-and-stomp fiddle hoedowns to mournful, heart-wrenching ballads of unrequited love; no holds barred, no punches pulled. Then, the kind of life out of which country music evolved and which it continues to represent speaks to those who practice or yearn for an uncluttered way of life—blue skies and blue jeans, a whoop of joy or an unabashed burst of tears, pure and natural emotions and settings. In a very real way, country music is a part of America's growing concern with honesty and living in harmony with nature.

Up to a few years ago country music remained more or less an isolated phenomenon. Northern fans were forced to point radio antennas toward Wheeling, West Virginia, Cincinnati, or Nashville to hear their favorite music. Now more than fifty per cent of the nation's radio stations broadcast country music, while Johnny Cash, Glen Campbell, and Jerry Reed have presented it on television. It has been used as the background score to many motion pictures, including *Bonnie and Clyde, Five Easy Pieces, The Last Picture Show*, and *Deliverance*. Singers of diverse backgrounds, such as Dean Martin, Ray Charles, and Tom Jones, also include it in their repertoires. Composers have used traditional rural melodies in symphonies and ballet works; rock music is infused with it. Country music is everywhere.

This book traces the development of country and western music back to its European and African antecedents. Settlers from the British Isles brought over ballads— lengthy narrative poems that related historical events, supernatural occurrences, and love affairs. Ballads were handed down by oral tradition from generation to generation and adapted according to a singer's tastes and personal experiences; the story line and setting were thus often changed to describe local events and places. The fiddle became the all-important instrument, on which musicians played ancient bagpipe and harp melodies and popular tunes. Although religious leaders viewed secular singing and fiddle playing as only a step away from original sin, colonists sang and played to while away the hours and retain communal ties.

Settlers who gravitated west into and across the Appalachian mountains continued to sing the old songs. Ballads became as inbred as families inhabiting isolated settlements, with only names and places changed. Music was an integral part of daily life. Women sang to make household chores pass more easily, while men let off steam stomping out fiddle tunes.

An equally important element of rural music remained along the Atlantic seaboard. Africans who were brought to this country as slaves adapted their own native music to their plantation work. Unlike solo Anglo-Irish ballads, African music made full use of group participation. Solo and chorus call-and-response, polyrhythms, and body movements led to songs for planting, harvesting, and other kinds of work. Traditional and improvised instruments provided the accompaniment for singing and dancing.

Increased rural mobility following the Civil War helped to integrate black and white music. On railroad crews and road gangs there was a steady exchange of melodies, rhythms, and chord progressions. The result was a fusion of mountain modalities and plantation rhythms.

Other regional and ethnic groups influenced country music as well. Spanish harmonies and meters joined Anglo-Irish melodies in cowboy songs about life on the range. Urban popular music trickled back to rural communities, again adapted by local banjo and guitar players.

Except for a fiddler attracting crowds to a medicine show, rural music had remained an amateur venture, performed on back porches and at barn-raisings for one's own and neighbors' entertainment. Then, early in the twentieth century, the advent of the radio and the phonograph record turned country music into a commercial industry. Producers scoured the hills for performers and were rewarded with the Carter Family, Jimmie Rodgers, and others. Families gathered around radios to hear weekly programs such as the WLS Barn Dance, Midwestern Hayride, and Grand Ole Opry. Hollywood capitalized on native music: Western films starred singing cowboys, and rural music became country and western.

The Depression and World War II spread country music throughout the United States, as Southern factory workers or barracks bunkmates introduced it to others. Recent years have seen country music as a cross-regional force. Simultaneously influencing and borrowing from other types of popular music, it spawned a new breed of performer and writer who chose country music as a vehicle to express the age-old themes of love and death, happiness and sadness. In keeping with more sophisticated lyrics, the music became more heavily arranged into what came to be called "the Nashville sound," but the original tradition continued. Rural musicians traveled to urban festivals and concert dates, attracting people to their kind of pickin' and singin', and involving many of them as participants.

Certain categories of lyrics will serve in this book to trace country music's evolution. The first section deals with love songs and emphasizes the British ballad tradition. Work songs focus on the contributions of blacks. The fusion of the two is the subject of the chapter on adventure songs, and the concluding section explores country music's influence on other forms and styles of music. No limitations across or within these groupings are intended, however; just as work songs include adventure themes, so people of all cultural and ethnic backgrounds have sung of love. Nor does the book's groupings imply that no other kinds of lyrics appear in country music. The subject of religious music, for example, deserves an entire study with respect to both its musical influences and the attitudes toward this and the next world expressed by its lyrics. Songs appearing within these three categories are representative of the hundreds of thousands of rural lyrics and their variations, and are chosen out of familiarity and personal preference. To avoid belaboring points with a surfeit of examples, additional songs on the same subjects are listed in the Notes and Discography.

TAKE ME HOME is also an appreciation, the author's attempt to share his enthusiasm for country music. The music of my teenage time and place had been 1950's rock'n'roll, with an occasional sortie into a high-school band's renditions of "In The Mood" and "Miami Beach Rumba"; my instrument was the guitar. During my freshman year in college I met a fellow who also played the guitar. He was interested in old-timey music and bluegrass. The tunes had a bright, bouncy quality that led me to strum along to songs on unfamiliar recording labels. The lyrics were appealing, with their "let's-dress-up-like-cowboys" exoticism—no one I knew came from the Blue Ridge Mountains, much less longed to return to the log cabins there, but somehow it sounded like a pleasant idea. So while I figured out G-chord runs, my friend raced out to buy a five-string banjo. I switched to mandolin and fiddle when another classmate learned to play guitar, whereupon dormitory neighbors strongly recommended that we practice in a fallout shelter across campus. Enter someone with a washtub bass and autoharp, and the Monroe County Digital Pyrotechnicians was born, four Yankees to whom, for all we knew, "Salty Dog" meant a defective frankfurter. With more enthusiasm than ability, we made our professional debut at a bar outside of town, a replica of a frontier saloon, whose patrons wore Western clothes and danced, drank, and brawled on Saturday nights. Our group scoured the area for country music concerts, going backstage to ask musicians to bless our fingerpicks.

Another freshman in our dormitory was away from home for the first time. He sorely missed his family, especially a pet dog. Tears welled in his eyes when he heard a recording of "Old Blue," an Appalachian ballad about a hound, and I got my first inkling of the sentimental aspects of country music.

Anecdotes and enthusiasm cannot, however, convince others to like country and western music. It is the music itself that provides the enjoyment. In that sense, this book is intended as a guide, perhaps bringing some to discover country music for the first time. Bear in mind, however, that the ear, not the eye, is the only real way to approach the subject; listening to country music is essential.

It might be useful at the onset to try to define country music or at least distinguish it from other kinds of popular music. Although it is folk music with respect to its artlessness, one should dismiss most of the ethnomusicologists' concern with "purity." Anything, rural or urban, foreign or domestic, which sounded good to country musicians found its way into their songbag. Nor is folklorists' preoccupation with "collective origins" (authorship shrouded in anonymity and antiquity) particularly germane. We know the identities of the writers of many if not most country songs—or, if they were not the actual writers, at least we know who made some sort of proprietary claim for copyright purposes.

How can we describe country music? First, it is rural-oriented, evoking the country. Lyrics are basic—"corny" according to some, but "real" and "honest" to others. Images are more visceral than cerebral; the verbal gymnastics of a Cole Porter or Lorenz Hart are as alien to country music as major 9th–flatted 13th chords. Melodies tend to be simple and straightforward within limited harmonic schemes of three or four chords. Performances, though polished, are marked by a relaxed and easy sound, even when the tempo is fast. There are certain vocal and instrumental conventions that help identify country music —the nasal quality of a singer's voice, or a familiar chord progression. Country music? You know it when you hear it.

1

A Red Rose and a Briar

LOVE SONGS

The hub of activity on Saturday nights in one small Texas town is a roadside bar. Too young to be admitted legally, teenagers congregate at a root beer stand across the highway, their car radios blaring rock music that clashes with the sounds coming from the roadhouse. Inside Cal's Hi-Ho Tavern, forty customers drink away most of their week's paychecks. The live entertainment that weekend comes from Eddie Jackson and His Pecos River Boys. The band is more than homegrown talent; they've been in the business for almost four years, making their way around the Southwest playing any date that (1) pays and (2) provides exposure. Maybe a talent scout or recording executive will be in the audience ready to offer a contract that will lead to the big time. For the moment, however, they simply follow their routine of performing a mixed bag of songs—some old-time standards, a few from the day's hit parade, and some written by members of the band.

It's close to midnight. The band returns after an unscheduled break. A fight had broken out at the bar—seems a feller from the next town took a fancy to someone else's girlfriend. After watching a few punches thrown, the bartender-bouncer walks around to separate the participants, then tosses out the stranger with a warning to "stay away or you'll end up looking like five miles of bad road!" It takes several minutes before tables are righted, customers retrieved from the doorway, and drinks set up again. Now it's the band's chance for attention. Instruments are replugged and retuned; the drummer takes one last drag on a cigarette and fishes around inside his shirt pocket for the phone number of that brunette, the one with the beehive hairdo and tight slacks who had gone backstage between sets. Eddie Jackson sips from a paper cup, puts it back on his guitar's amplifier, turns to the band, and nods out the beat to a slow tune:

> Your cheatin' heart will never weep,
> You'll walk around and try to sleep;
> But sleep won't come the whole night through,
> Your cheatin' heart will tell on you. *

A man at a bar, alone, leans lower over his bourbon and water, hands clasped around the glass, lips moving soundlessly. The bartender idly rinses beer glasses, trying to remember how often he's heard those lyrics. The fellow whose girlfriend provoked the fight emerges from the rest room, wipes his cut lip on a napkin, and yanks her to her feet. They join the other couples on the dance floor, barely moving in close embrace. No one in the room fails to react in some way to Hank Williams's lament for those who feel, or have ever felt, searing, painful, raw emotion.

Life in the frontier backwoods was dour and demanding. Great forests were punctuated by clearings where one-room log cabins shared space with hog pens, corn cribs, and farmed fields. Neighbors were too far away for anything but infrequent visits, and such isolation created a need for self-sufficiency. Settlers got their meat from the paddock or the forest, produce from gardens and

---

fields, tools and clothes from available resources and ingenuity. This isolation also shaped the settlers' music. They lacked both the leisure time necessary to carry on the cultivated tradition of classical music and the money with which to buy and transport classical instruments. To spend money on a harpsichord rather than on extra sacks of seed would have been a sacrifice of the greatest folly.

Among the kinds of freedom which settlers achieved was freedom of musical expression. A husband took full advantage of the distance between his homestead and the nearest church to ignore religious restraints against "the Devil's music." After a day behind a plow, he would pick up his fiddle, rosin the bow, and launch into adaptations of Scottish and Irish bagpipe melodies, fifteen- or twenty-note tunes readily fitted to the fiddle. A local bard might add couplets on almost any subject. The result was a repertoire of mountain reels and hoedowns as suitable for neighborhood frolics as for an individual's letting off a little steam:

> Goin' up Cripple Creek, goin' in a run,
> Goin' up Cripple Creek, have a little fun;
> Roll my britches to my knees,
> Wade in Cripple Creek when I please.

The music of pioneer women tended to be considerably less merry. While a husband looked forward to unwinding with an exuberant fiddle tune like "Old Zip Coon" or "Cumberland Gap," his wife filled her day with the old ballads of the British Isles. As she cooked, spun, or attended a neighbor's lying-in, she entertained herself with somber tales of love and death, which were chosen to reflect her own thoughts. Ballads were a frontierswoman's soap operas. Tied to a life of bearing children, backbreaking work, and subservience to her husband, she found her sole means of wish fulfillment and escape through the lyrics of the "old songs." An examination of several will show what pioneer women found appealing.

The Scottish border ballad "Johnny Faa" recounts the relationship between a band of gypsies (and one in particular) and a highborn lady. She heard their singing, took a fancy to Johnny, and sang:

> Go take from me my silk mantle,
> And bring to me a plaidie;
> For I will travel the world over
> Along with the Gypsy Laddy.

Her declaration of love revealed themes of escapism and death:

> I could sail the seas with my Johnny Faa,
> I could sail the seas with my dearie;
> I could sail the seas with my Johnny Faa,
> And with pleasure could drown with my dearie.

Her husband set off in hot pursuit only to learn of his wife's decision:

> Oh I could leave my house and land
> And I could leave my baby;
> And I could leave my own liege lord
> And live with the Gypsy Laddy.

But not without bloodshed, at least in the border version:

> There were fifteen valiant men,
> Black but very bonnie,

And they lost all their lives for one—
The Earl of Cassillis' lady

Known variously as "The Wraggle-Taggle Gypsies," "The Gypsie Rover," and "The Gypsie Laddy," the song was popular throughout the British Isles. It was sung in America as "Black Jack Davy," set to a sprightly tune, in which the hero convinced a sixteen-year-old married girl to run off with him, and she denied her husband with the words:

> Last night I lay on a goosefeather bed
> Beside my husband and baby;
> Tonight I'll lay on the cold, cold ground
> In the arms of the Black Jack Davy.

To be married and a mother by sixteen was a commentary on the female maturation process along the frontier. To leave one's house and family for romance evidently seemed a splendid suggestion to a woman as she wiped away lye soap fumes on a torrid summer's day.

What woman whose beauty faded at an early age from hard work and childbearing would not envy someone for whom a man would die of tertiary heartbreak? Pride and unrequited love are the themes of the most famous ballad in the English-speaking world, "Barbara Allen":

> In Scarlet Town where I was born,
> There was a fair maid dwelling;
> Made every youth cry "well-a-day,"
> Her name was Barbara Allen.
>
> 'Twas in the merry month of May,
> The green buds they were swelling;
> Sweet William on his deathbed lay
> For the love of Barbara Allen.

He sent his servant to the town,
To the place where she was dwelling,
Saying "Mistress, mistress come with me
If your name be Barbara Allen."

And slowly, slowly she got up,
And slowly she drew nigh him;
And drawing the curtain to one side
Said "Young man I think you're dying."

"Oh yes I'm sick and very sick,
And never shall be better;
Until I have the love of one,
The love of Barbara Allen."

"Oh ken ye not in yonder town
While drinking in the tavern;
You pledged a toast to the ladies fair
But slighted Barbara Allen."

"Oh yes I ken in yonder town
While drinking in the tavern,
I pledged a toast to the ladies fair
But my heart to Barbara Allen."

As she was walking o'er the fields
She heard the death bell knelling;
And every stroke it seemed to say,
"Hard-hearted Barbara Allen."

"Oh father, father make my bed,
Make it soft and narrow;
Sweet William died for me today
I'll die for him tomorrow."

They buried her in the old churchyard,
They buried him beside her;
And from his grave grew a red, red rose
And out of hers a briar.

They grew and grew o'er the old church wall
Till they could grow no higher;
And there they tied in a true love's knot,
The red rose and the briar.

In its structure as well as its story, "Barbara Allen" is a characteristic example of the ballad form. Ballads typically used repetition of words, phrases, and lines to heighten the emotional appeal of the narrative and to draw out the story.

Thirty stanzas long in the English original, "Lord Thomas and Fair Annet" (variants named the woman Ellender or Ellen) became considerably shorter in this country. The plot remained the same, however, a tale of family advice and regret. Thomas asks his mother whether he should marry Ellender or someone described merely as "the brown girl" (or "the nut-brown maid)". His mother opts for the latter: "The brown girl she has house and land/Fair Ellender she has none." "Oxen and cattle, too" pipes up a brother. Ellender attends the wedding where her beauty and finery so outshine the bride's own that the brown girl stabs her. After avenging the slaying, Thomas takes his own life. In one version he asks that Ellender be buried by his side and the brown girl at his feet; in another, Thomas and his true love are buried side by side, a birch springing from his grave and a briar from hers. As with many ballads, "Lord Thomas" caters to its audience's interest in opulence. Thomas's family may have counseled him in favor of the brown girl's money, but Annet/Ellender/Ellen was not exactly impoverished:

She turned around and dressed in white,
Her sisters dressed in green;

And every town that they rode through,
They took her to be some queen.

A frontierswoman in faded calico and homespun found in
such imagery another way to indulge her wish fulfillment,
in much the same way that *Women's Wear Daily* and
Vogue are popular with contemporary women who want
to know about jet set fashions.

Another favorite was "Little Matty Groves" (also known
as "Little Musgrove and Lady Barnard"). Matty is approached in church by Lady B., who invites him to dally
the night with her while her husband is away. Overhear-
ing the invitation, a page dashes off to inform his master,
who returns to find the couple *in flagrante delicto*. Con-
sidering the circumstances, Matty utters a rather auda-
cious retort:

"How now, how now," Lord Arling cried,
"How do you like my sheets?
How do you like my new-wedded wife
That lies in your arms asleep?"

"Oh, it's very well I like your bed,
It's well I like your sheets,
But best I like your lady gay
That lies but hain't asleep."

Famous last words—Matty is killed. But his spunk is infectious, for when her husband asked her whom she pre-
fers, she replies:

"Very well I like your cheek,
Much better I like your chin,
But I wouldn't give Matty Groves' little finger
For you and all your kin."

This tale of cuckoldry and its consequences places it at the head of a long line of country songs where cheating, guilt, and recriminations are so prevalent that infidelity appears almost something of a sacrament.

Still another household is disrupted in "The House Carpenter," the American version of "Jamie Harris" or "The Daemon Lover." A stranger asks a woman to come away with him and thus forsake her husband (the carpenter of the title) and child. Revenues from his ships will maintain her, he assures her. She goes through with it, but:

> They had not been sailing about two weeks,
> I'm sure it was not three;
> When she sat down and she did weep,
> She wept most bitterly.
>
> "Alas my love, why do you weep,
> Is it for gold and store,
> Or is it for your house carpenter
> That you will never see no more?"
>
> "I do not weep for silver and gold
> Nor do I weep for store,
> But I do weep for my darling sweet babe,
> The one I'll never see no more."

And she never did, for the ship sank. American versions did not maintain the superstitious overtones of the original, with its "daemon lover." There, the seducer was the ghost of a former lover. In another version the man is literally diabolical—he has horns and cloven hooves and speaks knowledgeably about Hell.

The unsuccessful attempts in 1715 and 1745 to restore the Stuarts to the throne forced Scottish Highlanders to migrate to the New World, where they settled in the Appalachians. Along with their bagpipes and fondness for malt whiskey, they brought the ballad "Bonnie George Campbell":

Hie upon Highland and law upon Tay,
Bonnie George Campbell rode out on a day;
He saddled, he bridled and gallant rade he,
And hame came his gude horse but nae hame came he.

Out came his bonnie bride plaiting her hair,
Out came his mother grieving full sair;
The corn is a-field, the wheat is unshorn
And Bonnie George Campbell will never return.

Generations away from kilts and sporrans, their descendants reworked the ballad into:

Georgie Collins drove home one cold winter night,
Georgie Collins drove home so fine;
Georgie Collins drove home one cold winter night,
Was taken sick and died.

The ancient "Fair Annie of Lochroyal" (or "The Lass of Loch Royal") came to this country as the tale of a woman setting out to locate her lover, the father of her child. She finds him with another woman and on the way home she drowns. What once was

"O who will shoe my fair foot
And who will glove my hand;
And who will lace my middle gimp
With a new-made London band?"

"Your father'll shoe your fair foot,
Your mother glove your hand;

> Your sister lace your middle gimp
> With a new-made London band."

became, in the spirit of feminine independence,

> "Oh, who's gonna shoe your pretty little feet,
> Who's gonna glove your hand;
> Who's gonna kiss your red ruby lips
> Who's gonna be your man?"

> "Mama's gonna shoe my pretty little feet,
> Papa's gonna glove my hand;
> Sister's gonna kiss my red ruby lips,
> And I don't need no man."

This ballad extols the move back to the warmth and security of one's parents and kinfolk, away from humdrum daily chores and the company of a preoccupied husband. But, the threat "I'm going home to my mother" was an empty one in the backwoods, since it would have required a trek of at least several hundred miles. So the threat was turned into song. Happy love songs were rare indeed, with two notable exceptions: "Pretty Little Miss (All in the Garden)" (or "John Riley") begins in the same fashion as "The House Carpenter," but the stranger reveals himself as his love's faithful betrothed. And "Froggie Went A-Courtin'" is a high-spirited song about a short-lived barnyard romance that ends mock-tragically when Mr. Froggie, Miss Mouse, and the wedding guests are "eaten up by a water snake."

With the passage of time and place, female escape fantasies became even blunter:

Single girl, single girl, going dressed so fine;
Married girl, married girl, goes ragged all the time.

Single girl, single girl, she goes to the store and buys;
Married girl, married girl, she rocks the cradle and cries.

Single girl, single girl, she's going where she please;
Married girl, married girl, baby on her knees.

Another song derived from a British broadside tells of a
girl who drowns herself rather than yield to connubial
pressures:

> I never will marry,
> I'll be no man's wife;
> I intend to live single
> All the days of my life.

As the frontier became more established, British lyrics
were further adapted to fit native customs. Names of
people and things were changed. Barbara Allen became
Barbary Allen or Ellen and lived in Charlotte, not Scarlet
Town; Matty Groves's rival was Lord Arlen or Lord
Arnold; the husband pursuing his wife and Black Jack
Davy ordered, "Go saddle me my buckskin mare," as compared to the "dapple" in the original. "The Cuckoo" was
transformed from:

> The cuckoo is a pretty bird,
> She warbles as she flies;
> She brings us glad tidings
> And tells us no lies.

into

> The cuckoo she's a pretty bird,
> She wobbles as she flies;
> And she never sings "cuckoo"
> Till the fourth day of July.

Another category of ballads shows that more than a broken heart could result from romantic entanglement. The outcome could be fatal, and not just by death from unrequited love. America's frontier was a violent place, inhabited by brigands and border raiders and unhampered by police forces. Any courtly concept of placing women on pedestals was left somewhere east of the Appalachians. Mountain and plains men took what they wanted. If the result of a tryst led to pregnancy, or if a man subsequently changed his mind about marriage or were himself spurned, these Lochinvars were fully prepared to indulge in a bit of bloodshed. The Appalachian favorite "Pretty Polly," sets the macabre tone of this genre:

I courted Pretty Polly the live-long night (twice)
And left her the next morning before it was light.

"Polly, pretty polly, come go along with me,
Before we get married some pleasures to see."

She jumped up behind him and away they did go,
Over the hills and the valley below.

They went a little further and what did they spy,
A new dug grave with a spade lying by.

"Oh Willie, oh Willie I'm scared of your ways,
I'm scared you will lead my poor body astray."

"Polly, pretty Polly, you guessed about right,
For I slept on your grave the best part of last night."

He stabbed her in the heart and the blood it did flow,
And into the grave pretty Polly did go.

> He put on some dirt and started for home,
> Leaving no one behind but the wild birds to roam.

The British broadside on which this ballad was based, "The Gosport Tragedy," concludes with the man trying to escape on a ship. Because the ship will not leave the port, its captain believes a murderer must be on board. His suspicion is confirmed when the ghost of Polly, babe in arms, identifies her killer. As in "The House Carpenter," however, this supernatural ending did not survive in America.

Songs of romance leading to murder carried on the ballad concept of chronicling events for neighbors and posterity. Many describe situations documented by courthouse and newspaper records. For example, "Naomi Wise" (or "Omie Wise") tells of the murder of the title character by one Jonathan Lewis in the early nineteenth century. He promised to marry Naomi, but when his mother finds him a more prestigious match, he takes his betrothed to a secluded spot and drowns her. "Tom Dula" (the original of the "Tom Dooley" popular in the 1960's) arose out of a slaying in North Carolina in 1866. Dula returns home after serving the Confederacy to discover that Laura, his boyhood sweetheart, has not remained faithful to him. What's more, the man with whom she has been keeping company is a *Yankee* schoolteacher. Laura errs when she takes a walk with Tom, from which she never returns. Legend has it that Dula composed the song on the eve of his execution.

In the many songs of this sort, the victims meet their fate in a variety of ways. "Naomi Wise" is drowned, and "Poor Ellen Smith" shot; "Banks of the Ohio," "Tom

Dula," and "Pretty Polly" are cases of stabbing, "Fatal Glass of Wine" poisoning, and "The Knoxville Girl" (a variant of the English "The Oxford Girl") bludgeoning; while "Rose Connolly" is poisoned, stabbed, *and* drowned. At the end of most of these songs, though too late to do much good for the dearly departed, the murderer usually professes true love, as in "Rose Connolly"—

> "Lo, Hell's now waiting for me,
> For I have murdered the girl that I love
> ▸Whose name was Rose Connolly."

—or confesses that unrequited affection moved him to kill, as in "Banks of the Ohio":

> "I murdered the only woman I loved,
> Because she would not marry me."

Women who grew up hearing these ballads claimed that they were sung as warnings to men who might make false vows. And if these songs, American tragedies in miniature, accurately reflected female reluctance and male violence, it is remarkable that frontier America was ever able to maintain, and in fact increase, its population.

❀❀❀

The musical settings for these songs underwent many of the same kinds of transatlantic adaptations as the lyrics. Performed by a solo vocalist unaccompanied by instruments, British ballads were sung to melodies using the medieval modes—somewhat different from the major or minor keys to which we are accustomed. Modal inter-

vals give an eerie quality to the melody, well suited to
ballads' dark tales of death and enchantment. (One can
get an idea of what modal music sounds like by listening
to Gregorian chants or Middle Eastern music. Much of
this sound can also be heard in traditional Appalachian
mountain music.) Almost one half of the ballads were set
in the Ionian mode, known to us as the C-major scale.
Other popular modes were the Mixolydian (C-major
octave with a flatted seventh) and the Dorian (C major
beginning on A with the F raised to an F sharp). Most
ballads were set in a high register. To produce these high
notes, vocalists sang from the larynx, which gave their
singing a shrill, nasal quality. The spread of church singing taught throughout the South in the nineteenth century
added harmonies of parallel thirds and fifths. The influence of Negro and urban popular music gave chordal
structure to country songs, placing them within the standard tonic/dominant/subdominant framework.

The frontier instrument was the fiddle. Popular in England, it came to America in the seventeenth century
where its portability and versatility made it a favorite
among settlers. The fiddle could duplicate modal sounds
as well as provide a range of musical emotion from the
seriousness of a funeral march to the high spirits of a
romp-and-stomp hoedown. The Scotch-Irish liked the way
the instrument could sound like a bagpipe; double-stop
techniques of fingering echoed the pipes' drones and mod-
al-melodic chanter. A story about Davy Crockett shows
the fiddle's place in frontier music. Following the sound
of a fiddle being played furiously, he discovered that it
came from a buggy stuck in a creek in the depths of a
Mississippi swamp. The driver, a minister, explained what

he was doing: "Here I was stuck in this torrent, ready to drown at any moment. I knew I could holler my lungs out and no one would come, but if I played me a tune on this devil's music box and there were a buckskin sinner in ten miles, he'd come a-trottin'!" For courting, a square dance, or a moment of solitary reflection, the fiddle com-plemented (and sometimes outdistanced) the human voice. It is no small coincidence that the first musician to perform on the Grand Ole Opry radio program was Fiddlin' John Carson.

❀❀❀

The extraordinary contributions that blacks made to country music included the emancipation of love songs from self-consciousness and social conventions. Unre-strained by white fundamentalist prohibitions against sex-ual enjoyment—and, in fact, often encouraged in such activity by their owners in order to increase a plantation's population—slaves sang bluntly about the pleasures of the flesh. Anglo-American lyrics alluded to carnal matters either through symbolism (red roses, briars) or euphe-mism (as in Pretty Polly's complaint, "I believe you have led my poor body astray"), but blacks sang about a wom-an's "custard-pie" and "jelly roll" and a man's "one-eyed trouser worm." Potency bravado and animal images abound:

> I been a mighty good bull cow, oh Lord,
>   but I got to go, (twice)
> I found me a pigmeat heifer, I can tell
>   by the way she lows.

Mama, I'm gone, with a horn as long as
your right arm,
And when I get to hookin', I'll have me
a brand-new happy home.

And,

I'm a king bee, baby, let me buzz around
your hive, (twice)
We can make such pretty honey, so let
me inside.

The phrase "easy rider," an expression commonly used in working with horses, shows up in many of these songs, where it has not only an 'in the saddle" sexual connotation, but refers also to a man living an easy life as a passenger taken care of by his woman.

But black love music is best known for the somber side of romance it evokes—the mean, mournful blues.* What is blues? "Nothin' but a good man feelin' bad," "a woman on a poor's man's mind," and "the difference between one and two." With its three-line stanza (the second usually a repetition of the first), the blues makes its point short and sweet:

It hurts to love a person that don't belong to you,
It hurts to love a person that don't belong to you,
"Cause when they find out you really love them,
they don't care what they do.

* The word "blues" did not originate with Negroes. An Elizabethan English expression "to look blue" meant "to feel blue." The derivation is thought to have come from the deep color of the sky after sunset when people seem most prone to melancholia.

In the wee midnight hours, long 'fore the
break of day, (twice)
When the blues creep upon you and carry
your mind away.

Generations of white people learned of Barbara Allen's
fickleness and Lady Barnard's infidelity through narrative
hearsay. The blues talked about the same kinds of events
and responses through direct, first-person involvement:

> If I was cold and hungry, I wouldn't even
>   ask you for bread, (twice)
> I don't want you no more, if I'm on my
>   dyin' bed.
>
> Every man in town knows about your
>   onery ways,
> Can't nobody change you now, 'cause
>   you've been a devil all your days.

Many blues lyrics focus on the end of an affair and the
hurt felt by the deserted party. A man might have left
for another, more attractive woman:

> I got a brown across town, she's as tall as a
>   sycamore tree,
> I got a brown across town, she's as tall as a
>   sycamore tree,
> Says she walked through rain and snow tryin'
>   to ease that thing on me;

or because of badgering at home:

> I believe I'll pack my suitcase, leave my home,
> I believe I'll pack my suitcase, leave my home,
> 'Cause every time I see my lil' woman, she's
>   got her gimmies on.

Even more than the man's, the abandoned woman's response is the quintessence of the blues:

I went to bed last night and the blues wouldn't
    let me rest,
I went to bed last night and the blues wouldn't
    let me rest,
"Cause I ain't used to sleepin' by myself.

Or,

Now, blues and trouble walk hand in hand,
Now, blues and trouble walk hand in hand,
I never had these blues until my best friend
    loved my man.

But life wasn't a bed of roses for the man, either:

I saw you ridin' 'round, you ridin' a brand
    new automobile.
I saw you ridin' 'round, you ridin' a brand
    new automobile.
Yes, you were sittin' there with your hustler-driver
    at the wheel. . . .
But I knew you was comin' home when you found out
    your driver didn't mean you no good.

If, however, she never came back, the man's thoughts
could return to his former woman:

But I seen my mistake after it was too late,
Yes, I seen my mistake after it was too late,
Well, I tried not to worry, "cause we're subject
    to mistakes."

Perhaps he went home to a loving, forgiving woman; perhaps she had found someone else. Conjecture can lead to
any number of conclusions, since the blues, rather than
telling the whole story, is more concerned with explaining

immediate condition and seldom does more than hint at resolutions.

There is less of a tradition here of songs about murder in the cause of love than in white ballads. Southern mores permitted blacks greater freedom to form and dissolve liaisons, so that murder as an alternative to a breach-of-promise lawsuit was not so frequent in black society. Moreover, it has been suggested that the specter of white jury verdicts (and their inevitable consequences for blacks—prisons and chain gangs) might have acted as a stronger deterrent to blacks than to whites. But not all blacks were innocent of crimes of passion. There is, for instance, the well-known "Frankie and Albert" (more popularly known as "Frankie and Johnny"). After relating what happens when Frankie discovers her lover "doing her wrong," the song concludes:

> This story has no moral,
> This story has no end;
> It only goes to show you
> There ain't no good in men.

It stands in contrast to the "I never will marry" notion of shunning involvement found in the white Appalachian ballad "Come All You Fair and Tender Maidens":

> Come all you fair and tender maidens,
> Take warning how you court young men.
> They're like the stars in the summer morning,
> First they appear and then they're gone.
>
> If I had known before I courted
> That love was such a killin' crime,
> I'd have locked my love in a box of gold
> And tied it up with a silver line.

The blues do not suggest that we overlook the consequences of romance. It warns us of the pain that careless love can lead to, but it tells us as well that to avoid emotion or to mask it in euphemistic terms is to overlook life's realities. Black love lyrics, candid in their revelations of personal pain and suffering, became an integral part of rural music in the nineteenth century and have remained a vital force ever since.

Another important influence on love lyrics came from the American cowboy. Perhaps because a ranch hand out West saw fewer females than Easterners did, his repertoire of love songs revealed a high degree of fantasy and reminiscence regarding women. The loneliness of cattle herding, where men went for weeks without seeing another biped, gave rise to lyrics like "Powder River":

> Last time on that old lazy river,
> When last I roamed its quiet shore,
> I met a girl who was more like heaven,
> And her smile will last forever more.
>
> Her eyes were of its deep blue water,
> And her skin was fresh as the dew on the leaf,
> And we fell in love right there on the river,
> But from its banks she would not leave.

The lovely "Colorado Trail" is evocative of imagery in Elizabethan ballads:

> Eyes like a morning star,
> Cheeks like a rose,
> Laura was a pretty girl,
> God Almighty knows.

> Weep all ye little rains,
> Wail ye winds wail,
> All along, along, along
> The Colorado Trail.

A woman's appeal did not always need to be physical in a milieu where one's value was determined by one's contribution to doing a job. Receiving high marks in that regard was "The Fair Lady of the Plains":

> There was a fair lady who lived on the plains,
> She helped me herd cattle through hard, stormy rains,
> She helped me one season through all the round-ups,
> She would drink with me from the cold, bitter cup.

Samuel Clemens called cowboys "Mexicanized Americans." Many came from south of the border, and those who grew up in the Southwest had been exposed to Mexican styles of clothing, horsemanship, and music. The influence of Latin romance—serenades under balconies amid roses riotously flung—may help explain cowboys' celebration of women, even when the object of their devotion was a whore. Whether the portraits they composed were accurate descriptions or merely bowed to convention, they introduced a strong Romantic element into country music.

There is at least one Western love song told from a woman's viewpoint, as rollicking as anything to come out of a bunkhouse after a wild Saturday night in town. "My Love Is a Rider" is attributed to Belle Starr, a cattle rustler who began her outlaw career as a spy for Quantrell's Raiders during the Civil War:

> My love is a rider, wild horses he breaks,
> But he's promised to give it up just for my sake;

One foot he ties up and the saddle goes on,
With a leap and a jump he is mounted and gone.

He made me some presents, among them a ring,
The return that I made him was a far better thing;
'Twas a young maiden's heart I would have you
	all know,
He has won it by riding his bucking bronco.

The two decades following World War I marked a fusion of the diverse lyrical and musical forces that have gone into the making of country and western music. Social mobility increased as employment opportunities opened up around the country. Depleted farm lands held no charms for young people, who like their settler ancestors, headed away from the family homestead to seek their fortunes. If a fellow heard of work in the city, he kissed his parents goodbye, told his sweetheart he'd be true, and headed north or west. But then the Depression spread across America as the Dust Bowl swept across the Southwest, and whether back home or away, people turned to drinking at roadhouses known as honky-tonks. Overlooked by local police and sheriffs, these taverns were places in which they could seek solace for a few hours or vent their frustrations in the brawls without which no Saturday night would be complete. As the whiskey sank slowly in the bottles, patrons clamored for sentimental songs that mirrored the losing hands they felt life had dealt them:

> When you are sad and lonely
> And have no place to go,
> Just come and see me, baby,
> And bring along some dough.

And we'll go honkytonkin' . . .
Honkytonkin' around this town.*

Love songs from this period have become standards in
country musicians' repertoires, and have spawned an entire line of sentimental lyrics in the blues' tradition of first-
person soul-baring. The traditional subjects of infidelity
and broken hearts are well-represented, as in Hank William's classic:

> Your cheatin' heart will make you weep,
> You'll cry and cry and try to sleep,
> But sleep won't come the whole night through,
> Your cheatin' heart will tell on you.†

It's a man muttering "you'll get yours" to a glass of beer,
as he tries to summon courage to confront his woman. Perhaps a "Dear John" letter has come from home or someone has told him that his sweetheart just married his best
friend—whatever the news, it's bad and his house of cards
collapses. Of course, the notion did not originate in this
era. A mountain ballad of the nineteenth century stands as
an abject antecedent:

> I wish to the Lord I'd never been born,
> Or died when I was young.
> I never would have seen your sparkling blue eyes
> Or heard your lying tongue.

> All the good times are past and gone,
> All the good times are o'er,
> All the good times are past and gone,
> Little darling, don't you weep no more.

So do "Short Life of Trouble" and "I Truly Understand (You Love Another Man)." Like the blues, these white songs describe a human condition as old as the hills. It's as fundamentalist as Southern religion—literal, all or nothing, heaven or hell, retributive: "You cheated and you're going to be sorry. I made a mistake, so you left." Every country and western radio station and stage show features these songs and their kin. The titles express the tone: "Cold Cold Heart," "Walking the Floor Over You," "(I'll Get Over You) When the Grass Grows over Me," "I'm So Lonesome I Could Cry," "Rainin' in My Heart."

Unlike Anglo-American ballads, full of conventions and refined collectively over hundreds of years, twentieth-century lyrics such as these are intensely personal statements that arose out of firsthand experience with despair, loneliness, and unrequited love. The life and work of Hank Williams are a prime example. Born in 1923, Williams was exposed to hymns and gospel music at an early age. When he decided on a career as a professional singer, he formed a band and toured the South, playing at whatever barn dances, honky-tonks, and radio engagements were available—starting at the age of fourteen. Williams got his break in 1947 when he began an association with Acuff-Rose publishing company and MGM Records. Both organizations recognized his extraordinary songwriting abilities and realized, too, that country-based music could be commercially successful across the United States. Williams's first gold record was "Lovesick Blues," a composition steeped in the Negro country blues of his native Alabama.

During this period Williams had been experiencing marital difficulties. He began to drink heavily to the extent that he was unable to perform at concert dates, and a back ailment required drugs to relieve his agony. These problems proved insurmountable; in 1952, Williams's marriage terminated in a divorce and he was fired from Grand Ole Opry. Rather than diminishing his musical output, however, these calamities inspired Williams to write some of his best songs: "Cold, Cold Heart," "Walkin' the Floor over You," "I'm So Lonesome I Could Cry," and "Your Cheatin' Heart," among others. The poignant lyrics came from the soul of a man racked by the worst kinds of pain, thoughts which men and women in similar emotional straits could clutch like a bottle of whiskey at midnight. The titles of two other songs—"I Don't Like This Kind of Living" and "I'll Never Get Out of This World Alive"— proved sadly prophetic. On the way to a comeback concert, Williams died on New Year's Day, 1953, from a heart attack reportedly brought on by alcohol and drugs.

❀❀❀

A woman in Nashville had come from Oklahoma to see her sister cut a record. During a lull in the session she told a stranger something about her life. She was twenty-two years old, having been married at seventeen, divorced at eighteen, remarried at nineteen, and divorced again a year later. Her first husband was so mean "he'd steal the eyes out of a dead cat." Spouse Number Two chased after anything in miniskirts. "What's ahead" she was asked. She shrugged, smiled, and admitted she still hopes that Mr.

Right will come along to appreciate what she can offer him—love, a good home, and children. Her story evokes a strain of contemporary love songs. It used to be that women on the frontier would dream of knights and gypsies who might whisk them away from their daily drudgery. But now that women have more independence, their songs center, curiously enough, on making the best of what they have. One can term the genre "daily survival"—the homebody approach to holding onto a man:

> When he comes home I'm cooking breakfast,
> I haven't slept a wink all night long.
> I've been layin' in bed thinking like a woman,
> Wondering if my man's been doing me wrong. . . .
> But when he loves me, he really loves me,
> Ain't nothing left for me to say.
> But when he loves me, he really loves me,
> He loves me all the way.*

Rayette, a character in the motion picture *Five Easy Pieces*, had such a vision. She was in love, however, with a man who had little respect for her. While he charmed another woman by playing a Chopin prelude, Rayette found solace in "Stand By Your Man":

> Sometimes it's hard to be a woman,
> Giving all your love to just one man.
> You'll have bad times, and he'll have good
>   times,
> Doing things that you don't understand. . . .

* HE LOVES ME ALL THE WAY. Words and music by Billy Sherrill, Norris Wilson & Carmol Taylor. Copyright © 1970 by Algee Music Corp., 65 West 55th St., New York, N.Y. International Copyright Secured. All Rights Reserved. Used by permission.

Stand by your man, give him two arms to
    cling to,
And something warm to come to when nights
    are cold and lonely. . . .
Tell the world you love him,
Keep giving all the love you can,
Stand by your man.*

A few modern love songs maintain older ballad themes. Men and women still see "the devil" in each other's eyes; one woman regrets the night she "let you hang my wings upon your horns." And for a narrative with an ambiguous ending, "Ode to Billy Joe" might have been a reworking of a murky Child ballad—what indeed did the narrator and Billy Joe throw off the Tallahatchee Bridge and why did Billy Joe commit suicide?

Listen to an hour or so of music on any Top Ten country and western radio station, and you'll discover that contemporary songs (as well as "country classics" of the past several decades) deal with just about every aspect of the heart under the sun. An outraged wife explodes, "Don't come home a-drinkin' with lovin' on your mind" while her husband ponders, "How much more can she stand and still stand by me?" Sometimes romance goes smoothly when it's "Easy Loving" or when a woman greets every new day with the proclamation that she's "The Happiest Girl in the Whole U.S.A." More times than not, however, life is grim indeed for the heroes and heroines of these songs. To make it through the night, they seek help from other people or the solace of liquor, or both:

> Honey, come in, sit down, won't you join me for
>   a round;
> I could use me a friend who understands;
> And look right here, you see it's printed on the can,
> No opener needed, if you're mine, then I'm your man.
>
> If you're mine, then I'm your man;
> It don't matter what I am,
> "Cause the only thing I need
> Is right here in my hand.
> And it's cold, but I'm warm,
> But it really ain't no sin,
> So there's no opener needed—if you're mine, then
>   I'm your man. *

Many of the most successful (that is, most popular) lyrics involve puns or plays on words. Repetitions of words or phrases often stand in counterpoint to each other to produce poignant effects. A representative song, not unexpectedly set in a bar, is "That Girl Who Waits on Tables":

> I watch her pickin' up their tips off the table,
> And see them smile as she brings another round.
> That dress she's wearin' shows she's all woman,
> And it reminds me I once had what they want now.
>
> That girl who waits on tables used to wait for me
>   at home,
> And she waited 'til all her love was gone.

The fiddle, for years *the* instrument of country music, is still popular among rural folk. *(Photo Researchers)*

Hank Williams *(Wide World Photos)*

Glen Campbell (above) and Dolly Parton and Porter Wagoner, whose renditions of country classics as well as contemporary ballads are recognizable to millions, have bridged the gap between traditional country music and popular music. (*Wide World Photos* and *RCA Records*)

Blacks on plantations
and small farms, mus-
ing on their condition,
created the blues.
(Photo Researchers)

The outlandish cos-
tume and stage patter
of Grandpa Jones are
in the tradition of the
nineteenth-century
minstrel show. *(Coun-
try Music Association)*

A rural railroad construction gang. *(Wide World Photos)*

There would always be at least one guitar in the bunkhouse of any ranch. *(Photo Researchers)*

I'm too late but I still worship the floor she's
    dancing on,
That girl who waits on tables used to wait for me
    at home.*

What then do country music's love lyrics tell us? Nothing more than anyone already knows. Romantic stability
is a sometime thing. If love, as well as life, is a vale of
tears, these songs direct us not to the next world but the
more difficult and immediate task of making it through
the nights and days. Phrases like "vale of tears" and "till
death do us part" are better left to sermons. Country music
has always seemed to care more about Saturday nights
than Sunday mornings.

2

A Hammer and a Piece of Steel

WORK SONGS

The rain started around Knoxville as a soft drizzle, then became a steady downpour as the truck weighed in at the North Carolina line. "It's going to be another one of those runs," the driver thought as he switched on the radio. Passing under high-tension wires, the cab filled with static. The driver found the end of a Midwestern baseball game, but the announcer's voice kept fading in and out. He switched to a local station. The whine of a steel guitar sounded like the whine of tires on the wet pavement. Between the hypnotic beat of the windshield wipers and the monotony of the road's sameness, he almost failed to see a car weaving toward him from the opposite direction. The beat-up car swerved at the last moment out of the truck's path, speeding by with the drone of a souped-up engine and glass-pack muffler. "Goddam kids," the driver muttered, "they oughta take driving lessons from their granddaddies—those old boys could outdistance tax men without spilling a drop of moonshine. Probably still doing it. Moonshine—still, ha-ha."

The driver slowed down a few miles ahead for a rail-road crossing. He had made this run maybe twenty or thirty times and there never was a train, but you can never be sure. There was this time. The grass around the tracks was high with no constant traffic to mow it. The last car of a freight train disappeared into the distance. "Sorry-assed caboose," he said to himself. "Railroads used to keep their rolling stock in good shape. Aw, that was years ago. Nobody uses trains these days. It's all trucks and airplanes. It's all up to people like me."

Passing through a town made him downshift again. A young man with a satchel and a guitar case stuck out his thumb. "Goofy-looking bastard. Besides, the boss would kill me if I took a hitchhiker." A diner loomed ahead two stop signs and a blinking light. The driver signaled, doubleclutched smoothly, and pulled into the parking lot. He pulled his jacket collar around his ears and trotted through the rain. As a waitress handed him a menu, the man threw a quarter into the jukebox in front of him. A punch of the buttons, a click, and on came:

> Well, my rig's a little old but that don't mean
>   she's slow,
> That's a flame blowin' from my stack, and that
>   smoke's blowin' like it's coal . . .
> Six days on the road and I'm gonna make
>   it home tonight.*

He had a ham sandwich, a slice of apple pie, and a cup of coffee, punctuated by some banter with the waitress˙ and followed by the luxury of a cigarette. Then it was back to the truck, with only a disc jockey and recorded music to keep him company as he disappeared onto the interstate highway and into the dusk.

Life is marked by rhythm. The progression from cradle to grave is composed of alternating patterns of activity and rest, sustenance and want, happiness and gloom. Less abstractly, people see their daily lives assuming the predictability of the changing of the seasons and, for most,

* SIX DAYS ON THE ROAD written by Earl Green and Carl Montgomery. Copyright 1963, Newkeys Music, Inc. and Tune Publishing Co. All rights reserved. Used by permission.

the monotony of a turning windmill. At the heart of this routine is the inescapable fact of having to work merely to obtain the basic necessities of food, shelter, and clothing. Rural life could not fail to recognize such spiritual and physical oppression. A person close to the soil saw himself in a rut as he planted, and then on a treadmill come harvest time. But those engaged in muscular labor discovered that the rhythms of their task could be used to advantage to lighten their burden and help them make it through the day.

Music was a fundamental part of African life. It was the backbone of myriad tribal celebrations—births, weddings, funerals, preparation for battle, thanksgiving for victory, fealty to chiefs, and welcomes to visitors. Like the rituals, the music was a communal experience. An African who performed solo or *a capella* would have been as unlikely a sight as a British minstrel who invited his audience to sing along with him. A tribe member holding a special status was the song leader. After first selecting what was to be performed during a celebration, he established the vocal lines, which the rest of the celebrants answered. The responses were not, however, mere repetitions. Melodies were embellished in a manner similar to Western theme-and-variation. Harmonic overlappings came when the chorus entered before the leader finished his line. Some of the singers, called "basers," added improvised grace notes, slurs, and soaring harmonies. A variety of instruments accompanied the singing. Horns, harps, flutes, bandoras (a kind of guitar), bells, and drums joined together in sophisticated interplay. Vocalists frequently sang one rhythm while wind instruments played another, and the percussion section yet a third. Everyone participated;

hand-clapping furnished additional rhythmic patterns and syncopation. Unlike Anglo-Irish ballads, which were sung in a rigid, restrained manner, African music required the total person. Body movements, dancing, and swaying were as much a part of the musical ritual as the audible sounds. European explorers who witnessed tribal events were astonished by such complete involvement, so different from their own staid state occasions and religious ceremonies. Try as they might, Europeans found it impossible to describe with precision these vocal and metrical complexities in terms of their own music.

Although the first shipment of Africans arrived in Jamestown in 1619, there was no widespread demand for slaves until the last decade of the eighteenth century. As the cotton gin spread "Whitney's disease" throughout the South, America's black population grew from 700,000 in 1700 to 4 million by 1860. Further importation of slaves was banned in 1808, but smuggling became a profitable way to increase the labor force. Farmers and plantation owners from Virginia to Georgia and the Mississippi delta discovered the value of owning slaves. Blacks of all ages, degrees of intelligence, and at least minimal health could work in cotton fields, as well as produce other staple crops of rice, indigo, and tobacco. There were relatively few very large slave holdings. Most farms or plantations had only two to fifteen blacks, so that a *Gone with the Wind* panorama of hundreds of field hands raising their voices like a bucolic Mormon Tabernacle Choir is less an accurate portrayal than a later era's fantasy.

The frontier pioneer who thought his life was impossibly demanding should have tried just a few hours as a slave. The difference was freedom. Blacks were chattels at the whim and mercy of their masters. An owner, especially on a small plantation, might have worked alongside his slaves, but more often the field hand's sole contact with the white world was through the overseer. And if this "captain" received a bonus on every bale of cotton harvested above a certain quota, that incentive led him to brutalize the workers under him. To reduce expenses, he permitted a diet of just a few mouthfuls of cornbread for breakfast, salt and cornbread or hominy (perhaps with some pork or bacon) for lunch; and a catch-as-catch-can supper after twelve or more hours at work.

Blacks turned to music to try to relieve the boredom of their backbreaking toil. Whereas a pioneer woman found escape in the lyrics of the ballads she sang, it was the rhythms of the slaves' music that helped make their conditions more bearable. With a steady beat to accompany him, a slave could lose himself in the repetitious motions of his work, carried along by the rhythmical pulse of his music much as his own pulse carried him along. The heritage of African music was the key, based on its tradition of communal participation. A solitary farmer along the frontier did not have the same incentive to sing as the blacks did, even though he performed many similar tasks. He could always put down his axe or hoe in order to rest or take a drink of water or just move on to another chore. A slave had no such option, and so he used his music to drive himself to keep ahead of the overseer's lash. Since few farms and plantations had only one slave, he usually worked in a group, as in Africa. There, tribesmen tilled fields while pacing their activities with improvised, accented songs. In America, one of the field hands, like his ancestral song leader, would select a tempo based on the work to be done. This beat was determined by the job—the yank of a cotton boll from the plant, the fall of a hammer or axe, or the stroke of an oar. The leader would voice a solo line, answered by other slaves in chorus and punctuated by the yank, thud, or pull of their work:

> Farewell, fellow servants, o-ho, o-ho;
> I'm going away to leave you, o-ho, o-ho;
> I'm going to leave the old country, o-ho, o-ho;
> I'm sold off to Georgia, o-ho, o-ho.

The "o-ho" marked the oars' strokes in this rowing song, as the slaves propelled a barge forward. According to a contemporary white man's account, the melody to the song was so plaintive and melancholy that female passengers on the barge were moved to tears. Work songs tended to be in minor keys, with intervals that resembled modal sounds. This all-pervasive plaintiveness was evident in "calls"—spontaneous, non-rhythmic, falsetto-like, wordless yelps and hellers from one slave that were answered by his neighbors. The abolitionist Frederick Douglass, himself a former slave, commented that the only time he heard such "wild" utterances was in Ireland during the potato famine, where women's wailing reminded him of plantation sounds.

Words to field and river songs were not as important as the patterns they created. An archetypical song survived in a Texas prison camp where it was used by black convicts at hard labor. Each line is repeated (and "grizzly" is sung with three syllables):

> Tell me who was the grizzly, grizzly bear,
> Jack O'Diamonds was the grizzly, grizzly bear,

He made a noise in the bottom like a grizzly bear,
Well, my mamma was scared of the grizzly bear,
Well, my papa went-a-hunting for the grizzly bear,
Well, my brother wasn't scared of the grizzly bear.

Heavy work was varied by "frolics" when slaves gathered to shuck corn or flay rice. One was selected to lead the singing. Perched on a corncrib, he or she would toss off lines followed by a fixed response:

> Hurray, hurray, ho;
> Round the corn, Sally;
> Hurray for all the lovely ladies;
> Round the corn, Sally;
> This lover's a thing that's sure to have you;
> Round the corn, Sally;
> He holds you tight when once he grabs you;
> Round the corn, Sally;
> An old, ugly, young, a pretty;
> Round the corn, Sally;
> You needn't try when once he gets you;
> Round the corn, Sally.

Verses could be nonsense and unrhymed, but occasionally the leader would concoct quatrains commenting on plantation life and liaisons that demonstrated the quick-witted skill of a calypso singer. The next day, a slave back in the field would appropriate a line that he found amusing or touching as the basis for another work chant. Overseers and owners encouraged all such singing, for even if they did not recognize its value in connection with productivity, by the sound they would determine their slaves' locations to and from work or in a large meadow or wood.

Free days—Sundays and holidays—did not include a respite from music. In addition to tending their own small gardens or mending clothes, hunting or fishing, blacks relaxed to the accompaniment of homemade instruments. A wooden hoop or gourd covered with animal hide and fitted with gut or leather strings became a banjo. Flutes and fifes were made from hollowed reeds. Skins stretched across logs or barrels served as drums. These leisure-time activities came closest to duplicating African traditions, as the plantation's entire black population (except, perhaps, for house servants who had risen above such "primitive" behavior) sang and danced in barns or around bonfires. "Patting Juba" was a complicated exercise in clapping and dancing somewhat like "Simple Simon."

A leader would set the tempo and give directions to the assembly:

> Juba left and Juba right,
> Juba dance with all your might;
> Juba here and Juba there,
> Juba Juba everywhere.

The company tried to outdo each other by mimicking the instructions and story lines; they put on an extraordinary display of syncopation, with simultaneous clapping, toe-tapping, and dancing steps in a variety of accents.

Slaves chosen as house servants had only a slight influence on black music. Encouraged to develop their musical talents, some were given flutes and violins with which they imitated the instruction given their owners' children. Brought back to the slave quarters, the music of Handel and Purcell and ballads such as "Barbara Allen" exposed Negroes to European tonal and chordal regularities. Time to develop their own music was limited, however. There was greater demand for slaves and servants to perform for whites. A black's musical ability was a source of value and identification: A slave who had instrumental training could fetch a higher price than an equivalent who had none, and runaways were often sought through advertising descriptions as, "Can play on the fiddle." (One common práctice was to force slaves to sing, dance, and play while being auctioned, callously disregarding the poignant fact that families were being separated.)

A plantation owner entertained his guests by showing his slaves "patting Juba" or shucking corn. The audience marveled not so much at the lyrics—often incomprehensible, since Africans coming from different tribes spoke a bastardized English—than at the rhythmic spectacle. "Barbaric madrigals" was one description offered by visitors who tried to place this exotic music in the context of their own tradition. As with European observers of African tribes, words failed them.

Stories of the slaves' virtuosity spread to the North. White professional musicians during the first half of the nineteenth century saw the opportunity for commercial exploitation, and travelled south to get a firsthand glimpse. They created their own songs and dances based on the plantation music and returned to urban areas to form minstrel shows. Wearing blackface and playing banjos, tambourines and castanets, they created the stock characters of Mr. Interlocutor, Zip Coon, and Jim Crow—the last based on a Kentucky stable hand whose limp evoked African syncopation. Minstrel shows gave Northern audiences the impression that Southern blacks led happy-go-lucky, shiftless existences—a distortion that was the subject of much criticism by anti-slavery forces. Lyrics, too, made life sound like a perpetual picnic, ranging from the sprightly description of "Camptown Races" to the geographic nostalgia of "Oh, Susanna," "Carry Me Back to Old Virginny," "My Old Kentucky Home," and, perhaps the most famous, "Dixie":

> I wish I was in the land of cotton,
> Old times there are not forgotten;
> Look away, look away,
> Look away, Dixie Land.

Black members of the troupe who had either escaped from the South or redeemed themselves from servitude did not comment on the truth of such conventions.

The music of the minstrel show was a dilution of plantation rhythms, housebroken for urban audiences used to European tonalities. There were certain elements of zesty Anglo-Irish fiddle tunes, but the main appeal was the sound of a steady bass supporting melodies with offbeat accents. Northerners who might never have heard slaves chopping wood or rowing in unison enjoyed adaptations of these workaday rhythms. It would be refined years later into ragtime and jazz, but in the era preceding the Civil War people flocked to see and hear the latest "Ethiopian opera" companies strut their cakewalks and "ring the banjo." Rural music had begun to make an impression on the city.

Another facet of plantation music that found its way into both black and white, urban and rural culture, was the blues, which came directly from work songs. Imagine a gang of slaves clearing a grove of trees. The leader begins with an improvised line, something like "Gonna chop all day at this live oak tree." As the others recover their axes for the next stroke, he repeats the words for emphasis (or for additional time to come up with another line), while altering the melody for variety and musical tension: "Gonna chop all day at this live oak tree." Then he resolves the lyric and melodic phrases with "I believe this live oak's gonna be the death of me." If the verse appealed to him and his companions, he would use it again another time. The first line would then be repeated so that other slaves, spread over the woods or fields, would be sure to hear it and join in on the last chorus.

Back in the cabin by himself, a slave would follow the same form for solo singing. Instead of a work beat, he would play banjo, fiddle, or guitar runs to mark the end of each line as an answering voice. The three lines were fitted into twelve musical bars and accompanied with a standard chord progression (tonic, dominant, tonic, subdominant, and tonic—as in the classic "St. Louis Blues"). He would heighten the musical tension by singing "blue notes"—the piercing, sliding, and moaning cries of field hollers—and would stretch the strings of his instrument to get these same agonized effects in his accompaniment. In both singing and playing, all the syncopation and improvisational flights of fancy of African music were retained. Off the plantation and through the years, the blues served as the basis for many different styles of music—ragtime and boogie-woogie, jazz, rhythm and blues, and, finally, rock-'n'roll.

❦❦❦❦

Work songs were not prominent in Anglo-American culture before the Civil War. British agricultural ballads had obscure origins in fertility rituals dating from Druid days. On leaving England, colonists were cut off from such village traditions as dancing around maypoles and chanting of the death of John Barleycorn—traditions which they saw no point in reviving in America. Sea chanteys for hauling mainsails and weighing anchors were, like plantation music, created for group labor and therefore unsuitable for the solitary farmer on the plains or in the mountains. This is not to say that whites never sang while plowing or harvesting, but simply that there is no body of songs at all comparable to that of the blacks. There were, however, songs about the farmer's condition, not so much work songs (that is, songs sung while working) as songs about work, sung during the farmer's leisure hours.

While his wife complained about the glamourless monotony of her life, the farmer had his own grievances. He had to contend with nature, whose severe winters could kill off his cattle, hogs, and sheep, and whose droughts, when there was no flooding, led to crop failure and loss of livestock. Irrigation was difficult on the plains, where wells had to be sunk often to a depth of three hundred feet. Insects and disease made periodic visitations. Transportation, essential to move crops and livestock to market (in the event he could produce more than just enough for consumption), was a problem, too: Railroad rates tended to be discriminatory and prohibitive.

With the influx of European immigrants throughout the nineteenth century, lands became increasingly populated, thus reducing the option of pulling up stakes when a homestead could no longer support a family. The Rockies stood as a barrier to western agricultural expansion, and cattle raising had claimed land up to the mountains; a "sod-buster" who tried to compete for these range areas invited confrontations and harassment by cattle ranchers.

It took a combination of stoic acceptance and good-humored irony to meet the problems of eking out a living.

> Ya know, I was born down there in the country on a little farm where the land's so poor that you got to put fertilizer around the telephone poles before you can talk over the wires.

In moments of conviviality, a farmer relaxed by scraping out a lively fiddle tune or joining in a barn-raising to the sound of another hoedown. But faced with low farm prices or the possibility of being served with a foreclosure lien, his attitude became caustic:

> My name is Tom Hight, an old bachelor I am,
> You'll find me out West in the country of fame,
> You'll find me out West on an elegant plan,
> A-starvin' to death on my government claim.
>
> Hurrah for Greer County! the land of the free,
> The land of the bedbug, grasshopper and flea;
> I'll sing of its praises, I'll tell of its fame,
> While starving to death on my government claim.

Of those who had taken advantage of the Homestead Act, some lost all hope of success and moved back East.

Newcomers brought with them the tunes that were popular in the cities they had left. A minstrel show ditty, "The Little Old Log Cabin in the Lane," was ruefully parodied into:

> I'm looking rather seedy now while holding down
>   my claim.
> And my victuals are not always of the best;

And the mice play shyly round me as I nestle down
   to rest
In my little old sod shanty in the West. . . .
And I hear the hungry coyote as he slinks up
   through the grass
'Round my little old sod shanty on the claim.

Falling prices after the Civil War, along with tariff barriers
and difficulty in securing credit, drove the fundamentally
independent farmer to join such organizations as the
Grange and the People's Party. Their theme song might
have been:

When the farmer comes to town
With his wagon broken down,
Oh, the farmer is the man who feeds them all.
Oh, the farmer is the man, the farmer is the man,
Lives on credit until fall,
Then they take him by the hand
And they lead him from the land,
And the middleman's the one who gets it all.

When the banker says he's broke
And the merchant's up in smoke,
They forget that it's the farmer feeds them all.

Sharecroppers of both races learned that the dual burden
of struggling against nature and working for another man
made earning a livelihood well-nigh an impossibility:

You go in the field and you work all day,
Wait the night but you get no pay.
Promised some meat or a little bucket of lard,
It's hard to be a renter out on old Penny's farm.
   It's hard times in the country, out on Penny's farm.

George Penny's renters they will come to town
With hands in their pockets and heads hanging down;
Go in the store and the merchants will say
"Your mortgage is due and I'm looking for my pay."
  It's hard times in the country, out on Penny's farm.

The Civil War and the resulting emancipation of slaves
did not bring immediate benefits to blacks. Merely telling
a slave he was a politically free man did not prepare him
to earn a living; "forty acres and a mule" was as much
propaganda as reality. Accordingly, most blacks found
themselves not much better off as freemen than in their
former state of servitude. Those who remained in agriculture became sharecroppers or tenant farmers, tied to the
land as closely as they had ever been. Former plantation
owners and banks advanced them credit for seed against
a percentage of the harvest, an annual syndrome from
which it was almost impossible to escape. Blacks who left
plantations learned that their only marketable talents were
at unskilled heavy labor—chopping trees, repairing roads,
and rowing boats exactly as they had been doing before
Appomattox. They became migrant workers for subsist-
ence wages. Whether members of turpentine and logging
crews, or of road, levee, and river gangs, they toiled con-
tinuously from sunup to sundown under the constant
threat of being fired. The same dismal conditions as
slavery prevailed, giving rise to the same reasons for singing. Africa or America, slave or free, the work and the
music remained the same.

Nothing did more to join black men and white men in
this tradition than the railroads. Following the great potato famine in the 1840's, the Irish came to this country
to work on the railroads and introduced or revived the

ballads and instrumental music of their ancestors. Fiddle
tunes buoyed the men's spirits around a campfire or in a
chantey after they spent the day blasting mountainsides
and hammering spikes. Reconstruction brought these
workers south of the Mason-Dixon line to build railroad
tracks and into contact with blacks who worked on the
crews. They felt an immediate affinity with each other's
music; after all, Irish reels and hornpipes were not far
different from the exuberance and syncopation of "patting
Juba." The Irish soon learned that to sing in unison while
working made the day pass more quickly. On the other
hand, the blacks earned the derogatory epithet "jig"
through their fascination with and adaptation of that Irish
dance form.

Working on all-male railroad gangs, men of both races
saw the heavy sledgehammers that they wielded in sex-
ual terms. The hammer was a potent extension of themselves, symbolizing tasks to be done by day and pleasures
to be enjoyed at night. Among the BaNyankole tribesmen
of West Africa, a blacksmith who acquired a new hammer
would try to insure its productivity by having relations
with his wife. Bakitara villagers carried an anvil fresh
from the forge as they would a bride in a wedding procession. In America, when anyone spoke of hammering,
the number-one man was John Henry:

> When John Henry was a little boy
> Sitting on his pappy's knee,
> He picked up a hammer and a little piece
>   of steel,
> Said, "Hammer's gonna be the death of me."

Some say he was born in Texas,
Some say he was born in Maine,
But I don't give a damn where John Henry
    was born,
He was a steel-driving man.

The captain says to John Henry,
"Gonna bring a steam drill around,
Gonna bring a steam drill out on the job,
Gonna whup that steel on down."

John Henry says to the captain,
"Lord, a man ain't nothin' but a man,
And before I let that steam drill beat me down,
Gonna die with a hammer in my hand."

The man that invented the steam drill
Thought he done mighty fine;
John Henry hammered fifteen feet deep,
The steam drill did only nine.

John Henry hammered at the mountain,
His hammer was striking fire.
He hammered so hard he broke his poor heart,
He laid down his hammer and he died.

They took John Henry to the graveyard,
They buried him in the sand;
And every locomotive comes roaring by
Says "There lies a steel driving man."

John Henry really did exist. He was a member of a black
crew working on the Big Bend tunnel along West Virginia's New River. Although the song's version of his death
is apocryphal (he was actually killed in a rockslide many

years after the Big Bend was completed), he was regarded
as a hero for many reasons. Above all, he demonstrated
the superior stamina of flesh and blood compared with an
impersonal machine. From a black man's viewpoint, he
bested the white man's contraption. And, according to
the song, he ended his life as any laborer sweating in the
fierce heat of a tunnel or under the burning sun would
have chosen—just sexually "hammering" himself to death.
Like all heroes of folk legends, he was a figure whom
others strived to surpass:

> This nine-pounder hammer,
> It killed John Henry,
> But it won't kill me.

That verse also appears in a work song where the hammer's fall comes after each phrase:

> Take this hammer, carry it to the
>   captain, (twice)
> Tell him I'm gone, boy, tell him I'm gone.

> This old hammer killed John Henry, (twice)
> But it won't kill me, no it won't kill
>   me.

Once construction had been completed on railroads
across the South, attention focused on locomotive engineers for whom fatality brought fame. Drivers' fanatical
devotion to meeting schedules—to the point of risking their
lives—was chronicled in ballads like "The Wreck of the
Old 97":

> They gave Steve his orders in Monroe,
>   Virginia,
> Saying "Steve, you're way behind time;

This is not 36, it's the old 97,
You must get her into Danville on time."

Steve turned around to his greasy fireman,
Saying "Shovel in more coal;
For when we hit that White Oak Mountain
You will see 97 start to roll."

They were going down the track doing
    ninety miles an hour
When the whistle began to scream;
Steve was found in the wreck with his hand
    on the throttle,
He was scalded to death by the steam.

In 1890 a landslide near Hinton, West Virginia claimed the life of George Alley as he piloted the Chesapeake & Ohio's #143, the "FFV" ("Fast Flying Vestibule"):

Along came the FFV, the swiftest on the
    line,
Rolling down the C&O road just twenty minutes
    behind,
Rolling down the C&O, headquarters up the line,
Receiving her strict orders from a station just
    behind.

Up the road she darted, into a rock she crashed,
Upside down the engine turned, poor Georgie's
    head was smashed,
His head was in the firebox found, the flames
    a-roaring high,
"I'm proud to be born an engineer, on the C&O
    road to die."

These songs were set to tunes that were well-known along the right-of-way, often church hymns.

"Casey Jones" tells the story of John Luther Jones, whose hometown of Cayce, Kentucky, provided his nickname. He gained immortality in the manner of a ship's captain who voluntarily went down with his vessel. Someone on the Illinois Central either was asleep at the switch or else did not take into account Jones's penchant for speed. As his train overtook another in the process of being shunted off the main track:

> He pulled up within two miles of the place,
> Number Four stared him right in the face;
> He turned to his fireman, said "Jim, you
>   better jump,
> 'Cause there's two locomotives that are going
>   to bump."

Jones was equally renowned for his skill with a steam whistle: It was said of Casey that he could make a whistle moan "like a lonesome turtle dove." Engineers became identified with the distinctive pitches and cadences of the whistles on their locomotives, and many people knew which driver was coming through simply from the warning signals they heard:

> The switchman knew by the engine's moans
> That the man at the throttle was Casey Jones.

It was not unusual for an engineer transferred to a new locomotive to dismantle a favorite whistle and take it along with him.

Country music took on these lonesome sounds as a symbol of personal troubles. They fit into the blues like the wails of field hollers:

You oughta hear the K.C. when she
    moans, (twice)
She's moanin' like my woman when I'm
    gone.

A vibrato on a guitar string or a slide up a fiddle neck
approximated the sound:

Went down to the depot and looked upon
    the board, (twice)
It read, "Good time, children, but better
    down the road."

Railroading had a very special meaning for rural people.
It meant escape, whether by the "Underground Railroad"
or by passenger and freight lines that tenant farmers and
sharecroppers hoped might someday take them away from
their unhappy conditions. A railroad represented freedom
to men behind bars or lock-stepped on a chain gang: Inmates of a Texas penitentiary saw the headlight of the
"Midnight Special" shine through their windows. The
contemporary "Folsom Prison Blues" begins:

Hear the train a-comin',
It's rolling 'round the bend,
And I ain't seen the sunshine
Since I don't know when.*

Almost every hobo song alludes to endless tracks and riding the rods; the tune for "Casey Jones" is from an older
song that opens with the words:

* FOLSOM PRISON BLUES by Johnny Cash. Copyright ©
1956 by Hi Lo Music. All rights administered by Hill and Range
Songs, Inc. Used by permission.

Monday morning it was pouring rain,
'Round the curve come a passenger train;
On the blinds was Hobo John.

Country folk gave names to trains—*Yellow Dog, Shorty
George, Nancy Hanks,* and assorted *Cannonballs*—and
sang about them in familiar terms:

> *Flying Crow* leaves Port Arthur, calls at
>   Shreveport to change her crew, (twice)
> She will take water at Texarkana, yes,
>   boys, and keep on through.

Railroads were blamed for taking away lovers:

> Well, the *Bob Lee Junior* passed me with my
>   baby all on the inside, (twice)
> And the conductor said, "I'm sorry, buddy, but
>   your baby she got to ride."

When no emotional baggage was involved, these iron
horses were celebrated as objects of admiration:

> Look a-yonder comin', boy, she's making time,
> That old engine's burning up the rail, rail, rail;
> Headin' for the mountain that she's gotta climb:
> Bringing in the Georgia Mail.
>
> Ninety miles an hour and she's gainin' speed,
> Oughta put that engineer in jail, jail, jail;
> Has she got the power I'll say, yes, indeed:
> Bringing in the Georgia Mail.

The harmonica, known in the South as the mouth organ
or French harp, could imitate a locomotive's chugging as
well as its yelping whistles. So could the fiddle, as demon-

strated in the classic "Orange Blossom Special," where slides and rapid bowing transforms the instrument into a steam engine at full throttle.

Railroading provided one of the catalysts for the enormous success of Jimmie Rodgers. Born in Mississippi in 1897, Rodgers, like Hank Williams, was exposed to the vocal and instrumental styles of Southern blacks. Unlike Williams, however, he did not choose music as the first means of earning his livelihood. Attracted by the lure of railroading, Rodgers was first a water boy, then a brakeman traveling around the South and Southwest. He took his guitar along, entertaining other trainmen and anyone else who cared to listen, while learning songs and instrumental styles along the way. Rodgers was forced to retire from railroading at the age of twenty-eight when he was weakened by tuberculosis. He then turned to singing as a career. While touring with a medicine show band in 1927, he answered an advertisement to audition for Victor Records (the Carter Family auditioned the same day). The rest became recording history. People flocked to buy Rodgers's records even when money was scarce during the Depression. His songs harkened back to "The Singing Brakeman"'s earlier life: "Waiting for a Train," "Will There Be Any Freight Trains in Heaven?," and "Hobo Bill's Last Ride." His series of "Blue Yodels" were marked not so much by the Alpine variety of yodeling as the sound of plantation field holler wails or train whistles. Accompanying himself on the guitar, Rodgers sprinkled lyrics with spoken phrases like "play that thing" or "hey, sweet Mama" as he picked out instrumental melodies.

Despite moving to more favorable climates in North Carolina and Texas, Rodgers continued to be plagued by tuberculosis, to which he succumbed in 1933. Rodgers's impact continued long after his death, through his own songs and through the careers of a number of people who, influenced by his example, became professional singers themselves—including Hank Williams, Gene Autry, and Ernest Tubb.

❀❀❀

Railroads created a demand for coal, because coal could power boilers more efficiently than wood. Mined in the Appalachians of West Virginia and Kentucky, coal became the most important factor in the lives of many of this area's inhabitants. Their songs describe the conditions under which they suffered, and they paint an unmitigatedly black picture. It would have been difficult, however, to make mining appear glamorous. The unrelenting boredom of a lifetime in the shafts and the ever-present dangers of cave-in were at the heart of a miner's life. Faced with clouds of coal dust and intense subterranean heat, miners had little incentive to waste air by singing. Moreover, little of the work was done in unison. At the end of a day a railroad crew might point with pride to having completed a stretch of track or plantation slaves to having marked a fully cultivated field, but the coal miner saw just a Sisyphean future. Little wonder that when a miner surfaced and washed off the dust, he would want to sing about anything other than his livelihood.

A West Virginian recalled that in his youth, "People worked fifteen hours a day, loaded a four-ton car, they'd get a dollar out of it. If a company could, it'd take that. . . . One time they hauled a mule out. They fired the guy that got that mule killed. They told him a mule's worth more than a man. They had to pay $50 for a mule, but a man could be got for nothing."* One song warned against such a life with these words:

> Come all you young fellows, so brave and so fine,
> And seek not your fortune way down in the mine;
> It'll form as a habit, seep into your soul
> 'Til the blood of your body runs as black as the coal.

> For it's dark as a dungeon and damp as the dew,
> Where the dangers are double and the pleasures
>   are few;
> Where the rain never falls and the sun never shines
> It's dark as a dungeon way down in the mines.†

❀❀❀

Cowboys also sang at, and about, their work. After the Civil War, men from all over the country headed west where cattle had begun to take the place of buffalo on the Great Plains and the foothills of the Rockies.‡ Former Confederate soldiers, freed slaves, disillusioned Midwestern farmers, European immigrants, and others arrived to

---

* From *Hard Times: An Oral History of the Great Depression*, by Studs Terkel. Copyright ©1970 by Studs Terkel. Published by Pantheon Books/A Division of Random House, Inc. Used by permission.

† DARK AS A DUNGEON. Copyright 1947 by Hill and Range Songs, Inc. Elvis Presley Music, Inc., Gladys Music, Inc., and Noma Music, Inc. All rights administered by Hill and Range Songs, Inc. Used by permission.

‡ Now almost exclusively associated with the West, the word "cowboy" dates back to America's colonial days. New Englanders who tended herds had the reputation as rowdy ne'er-do-wells, and bands of prowling Tories during the Revolutionary War were called cowboys by their detractors.

seek their fortunes and sometimes to escape the law. Few questions were asked about a man's past; the only important questions were whether he could sit on a horse and handle a lasso. A newcomer's skills were measured against standards set by Mexicans and Texans who were tough as longhorns, able to turn broncos into cutting horses and good at keeping a herd together on long trail drives to railroad loading points (or all the way to slaughterhouse centers). A good ranch hand needed not only a healthy dose of stamina to weather blizzards, droughts, and floods, but an ability to outguess cattle. A coyote's scent, a lightning bolt, or mere bovine orneriness could cause a stampede, endangering not only a cowboy's life but the lives of the cows as well, and therefore the total weight of the beef on which profits and wages were reckoned. One way to soothe horses and cattle, as people who work around livestock know, is with the human voice. Cowboys who rode nightherd on the open range circled around steers and crooned lullabies such as this one:

> Slow down, dogies, quit your roving around;
> You've wandered and trampled all over the
>   ground;
> Oh, haze along, dogies, feed kinda slow;
> And don't be forever on the go.

The animals' answering lows touched off feelings in the nightherder in ways that a train whistle affected a Southerner. The solitude of his surroundings evoked childhood memories, as expressed in this freely moving, mournful song, "Poor Lonesome Cowboy":

> I ain't got no father, (three times)
> To buy the clothes I wear.

I ain't got no mother,
To mend the clothes I wear.

I ain't got no sister,
To come and play with me.

I'm a poor lonesome cowboy,
And a long ways from home.

By day, song rhythms imitated a horse's gait. The familiar "Get Along Little Dogies" is in the waltz tempo of a three-beat lope or canter:

As I was a-walking one morning for pleasure,
I spied a young cowboy a-riding along.
His hat was thrown back and his spurs were
    a-jingling,
And as he approached he was singing this song:

Whoopie-ti-yi-yo, get along little dogies,
It's your misfortune and none of my own;
Whoopie-ti-yi-yo, get along little dogies,
For you know Wyoming will be your new home.

The Chisholm Trail ran from western Texas to Abilene, Kansas, to meet the Union Pacific's loading center. The trail was a well-trodden route along which cattle drives transported several thousand head over land and through rivers, averaging twenty miles on a good day. Under the supervision of a trail boss, cowboys kept the herds moving and watched out for rustlers and natural disasters. A good way to pass the time was to devise couplets to a song, whose lilting 4/4 rhythm complemented the sound of trotting hooves.

Oh, come along boys and listen to my tale,
And I'll tell you of my troubles on the Old
    Chisholm Trail.
Chorus: Come-a-ti-yi-yippi-yippy-yay, yippi-yay
Come-a-ti-yi-yippi-yippi-yay.

Woke up one morning on the old Chisholm
    Trail,
A rope in my hand and a cow by the tail.
(*Chorus*)

Cloudy in the East and it looks like rain,
And my damned old slicker's in the wagon
    again.
(*Chorus*)

Ten-dollar horse and a forty-dollar saddle,
Gonna quit punchin' those Texas cattle.
(*Chorus*)

"Whoopie-ti-yi-yo" and "Come-a-ti-yi-yippi-yippi-yay"
were cattle calls, exuberant yells used to attract the steers'
attention and urge them forward. Familiar to almost
everyone, the calls made fine choruses in which everyone
could join.

Other lyrics celebrated the Westerner's prowess. Along
with praising his own abilities, a cowhand liked to poke
fun at dudes who might think a saddle horn was used for
riding in traffic. But in "Zebra Dun" the joke is on the
veterans. A stranger's clothes and vocabulary mark him
as a tenderfoot until his riding an outlaw dun horse wins
the spectator's respect. The moral is quite clear:

There's one thing and a sure thing I've learned
    since I've been born—
Every educated feller ain't a plumb greenhorn.

The narrator of "TheTenderfoot" learns the hard way that ranching is not as glamorous as dime novels described it to be. After causing a stampede and being thrown from a bronco, he is given the choice of continuing the job or walking back to town:

> I've traveled up and I've traveled down,
> I've traveled this country round and round;
> I've lived in city and lived in town,
> But I've got this much to say:
> Before you try cowpunching, kiss your wife,
> Take a heavy insurance on your life,
> Then cut your throat with a Barlow knife,
> For it's easier done that way.

Coming from diverse backgrounds, cowboys had no common musical heritage. As a result, they developed a style of music from a mixture of various styles. Most songs were parodies of older ballads or popular ditties from back East, to which entirely new words were set. Church hymns suited nightherding songs and others of slower tempos. From the Southwest came Mexican waltzes and two-steps, while the British contributed hornpipes and reels. Although there were many blacks on Western ranches, plantation music did not have much of an influence on work songs out West, probably because ranching chores did not require accented, choral music.* Singing was usually unaccompanied. A fiddle or harmonica player in a bunkhouse or on the range was a rare phenomenon, and tolerance for someone learning to play an instrument was extraordinary. As in the East, a fiddler became an entire

---

* Plains Indians' ritual chants and dances sounded like gibberish to white men and thus had no effect on cowboy music.

dance band, sometimes even audible above the gunshots and screaming as cowhands squandered a season's pay in saloons and bordellos at the end of a cattle drive. Ranching was a life of extremes, and the work songs showed it.

American rural music is known as country and western, and the impact of the cowboy's music resulted in the addition of that second adjective during the 1920's. Jimmie Rodgers's great popularity as a country singer led others to imitate his outfits—high-heeled boots, fringed shirts, and Stetson hats. The costumes went right to America's heart. The nation had been smitten by the Wild West, from dime novels and Buffalo Bill's spectacles to William S. Hart's movies. "Hillbilly' meant "yokel" to urban audiences, leading promoters to seize on Rodgers's cowboy mystique to try to make other rural performers more palatable to them. Southerners like Hank Thompson and Ernest Tubb appeared in Western-inspired clothes, setting a sartorial trend that is still popular. Even some bluegrass musicians wear wide-brimmed hats and string ties while doing traditional Appalachian music.

When motion pictures became "talkies," the cowboy hero paused to woo his boss's daughter with a song, accompanied by musicians mysteriously but conveniently heard from behind the nearest cactus. Will Rogers discovered an Oklahoma telegraph operator who sang Jimmie Rodgers's songs pretty well, a fellow named Gene Autry. Hollywood provided Autry, Roy Rogers, and others with sentimental lyrics glorifying the West, women, and horses. These songs were mentholated imitations of authentic ranching songs with none of the originals' brand of irony and humor. But through exposure to the movies' singing cowboys and Southern performers in ten-gallon hats, the nation learned to like country and western music.

❀❀❀

Machinery is now involved in almost every phase of agriculture. The *Wabash Cannonball* has long since made its final run, leaving whatever romance that remains of American railroading to commuter trains. Jeeps and helicopters share stabling facilities with ranch horses, while cattle drives are conducted in trucks these days. Such automation has cut into employment for the nation's rural population, to the extent that thirty million of them have moved to urban areas over the past decade. Appalachian communities speak of the "graduate Friday—leave Saturday" syndrome of their young people. The Midwest is similarly affected; the federal government estimates that close to one million farms will disappear by 1980 as automation continues to make small holdings impractical.

Those who relocate to cities discover how debilitating unemployment is. Forced to accept welfare, they encounter not only a loss of self-esteem but antipathy from their new neighbors. In the country, they could enjoy solitude, but urban bright lights, which seemed so glamorous on television and in the movies, reflect only raw loneliness. One North Carolina teenager living in Washington, D.C. said, "I have no relatives up here—I'll always be lonely and think about home."

These are not the conditions under which work songs are created. Laborers on modernized farms and ranches find little to rhapsodize about; there is hardly an impetus to turn out something like "I ride an old jeep/and fly a light plane/And watch Allis-Chalmers/a-gather in the grain." Displaced country people manning assembly lines, who begin to feel like Charlie Chaplin in *Modern Times*, try to forget their lot in songs such as the nostalgic "Detroit City":

> By day I make the cars, by night I make the
>   bars . . .
> So I think I'll take my foolish pride and put
>   it on the southbound freight and ride,
> And go back to the loved ones, the ones I
>   left waiting so far behind. . . .
> Oh, how I wanna go home.*

It would be inaccurate to conclude a discussion of work songs without mentioning that there is an occupation that is praised in contemporary country music. Truck driving ballads sing the praises of the men who wrestle monster diesel semis around hairpin turns and along interstate turnpikes. Steering wheels and gearshifts may not look like nine-pound hammers, yet the whine of tires and metronome beat of windshield wipers evoke in drivers the same bravado as railroad engineers:

> ICC is a-checkin' on down the line
> I'm a little overweight and my logbook's
>   way behind;
> But nothing bothers me tonight,
> I can dodge all the scales all right,
> Six days on the road and I'm gonna make
>   it home tonight.

* DETROIT CITY Copyright ©1962 by Cedarwood Publishing Co., Inc., Nashville, Tennessee. Used by permission.

Well, my rig's a little old but that don't mean
    she's slow,
That's a flame blowin' from my stack, and that
    smoke's blowin' like it's coal . . .
Six days on the road and I'm gonna make
    it home tonight.*

Harvesters, trail herders, trainmen, and truckers sang as they worked about the prospect of enjoying moments of peace and rest, and their momentum carried them toward the company of familiar and appreciative people, in a sense kinfolk. Little wonder their thoughts turned to home.

3

I'm Stuck in Folsom Prison

ADVENTURE SONGS

No one had to tell the kid that he was good, he knew it himself. At least that's what folks back home said about his guitar-playing and songwriting. He had been spending all his spare time for the past six years listening to records and the radio, learning to duplicate Top Ten hits. He still preferred to do his own songs, basking in the applause and favorable comments at talent shows or amateur nights held at schools and churches. It might have been because his uncle owned a bar that the kid got a chance to perform there, yet there was no nepotism involved when the leader of a band on the same bill complimented him on one of his own songs. It was the summer after his graduation from high school. The kid knew he had to make his move. With a notebook of songs, his guitar, and a small suitcase, he hitched to Nashville—"Music City U.S.A.," where he knew he couldn't fail to set the industry on its ear. Not that anyone in Nashville called him bad. In fact, the few recording executives and music publishers for whom he auditioned had said, "Not bad, feller." Although they all rather liked his melodies and lyrics of love, sadness, and peace, as one publisher told him, he lacked that indefinable, special quality that made a star. "But keep plugging," he was told.

And plug he did. Up early every morning, he made the rounds of places on Music Row, following up leads, recommendations, suggestions. At first he was shy about asking to see people whose records he had heard all his life, then when desperation increased his boldness, the kid marched into offices, gave his name to secretaries, and waited in reception areas, reading trade magazines and papers he'd seen in other places all week. At the end of the day, he went back to his room, showered, changed his clothes, then set out for restaurants, bars, and clubs, hoping to meet someone—anyone—whose influence or inside information would lead to an interview or an audition.

The kid had been so sure that he'd make it quickly that he ran through all his money. After two weeks, a boardinghouse replaced the motel, and take-out stands, the more expensive diners and restaurants. Hanging around places where music people congregated wasn't cheap either—even beers at the bar added up. He decided to take a job —janitor/night watchman at a recording studio—where he thought he could rewrite and polish his songs when no one would catch him off duty. But the combination of pounding the pavements by day and working at night was too much. He fell asleep on the job and, as luck would have it, a valuable tape recorder was missing the next morning. The police came and questioned him; they released him, but he was fired.

Unable to get another job, too proud to write home, too broke to stay in Nashville, the kid hitched home. No recording contract, no flashy car, nothing to show for his month in Music City but a souvenir ashtray, a set of new guitar strings, and a pile of disappointments. And that wasn't the end of his adventures or his bad luck. The next evening, standing on a road in western Kentucky, he accepted a ride from a man who asked him to drive for a spell. Several miles later the kid swerved to avoid hitting a dog and sideswiped an oncoming pickup truck. No one was hurt, but the truck's load of live chickens was scattered all over the landscape. The highway patrol dis-

covered the car's owner had improper registration and no insurance, and, due to the lateness of the hour, suggested that the owner and the kid spend the night in jail until the matter was straightened out.

So there he was, the next Dylan-Cash-Kristofferson, behind bars, sharing a cell with the town drunk. He wasn't exactly in a maximum security penitentiary, but as the kid lay on a cot staring at a bedbug that wandered across the floor, he found himself humming:

> I'm stuck in Folsom Prison, and time
> keeps draggin' on.*

It scarcely required a Presidential commission to point out that America has always been a violent nation. Public moralizing to the contrary, people have for generations been fascinated with the outlaw living on the brink of or beyond social and legal conventions. To confirm this, one need only look at the popularity of books and films about gangsters, or the bloodlust in the eyes of the spectators at roller derbies and professional wrestling events. Movies with tepid sex scenes are given "R" ratings, while films that drip with blood and gore command public attention and even approval, as if maiming and killing should be an everyday part of our lives. It has been suggested that part of our attraction to outlaws might be attributable to a hidden desire to emulate their behavior. Of course we'd never do it ourselves—oh, perhaps weasel a little on an income tax return or make a prohibited U-turn on a deserted street, at midnight, when no one was looking, but never anything where there would be a great chance of being caught. Another reason for this attraction is our not-so-well-hidden penchant for escapism, wherein we are not so different from those pioneer women who sought refuge from boredom and hardship in the stories of the old ballads they sang. According to the dictates of society, one is supposed to settle down, do an honest day's labor for an honest day's wage, and find fulfillment as a credit to family and community. This attitude may do wonders for the gross national product, but there seems to be something in the human spirit which rebels against such a formula for programmed existence. Our admiration goes out to the maverick who is not fettered to farm, filling station, or executive suite. He is a mover and a doer, his own man for his own reasons.

This spirit of mobility and rebellion is deeply rooted in America's history, beginning with its founders—the Puritans and Quakers, transported convicts, entrepreneurs, freebooters, people who came to America out of persecution or restlessness. Their descendants resorted to force of arms to gain political independence. For every acre obtained by treaty and purchase, others were gained by fighting. Debates and compromises yielded to a Civil War in an attempt to settle political and social issues that are still with us. The frontier acted as a safety valve, but when there was no more available land, people looked to escape to the air, then into outer space. Movement—action, flight, pursuit—was also a musical *leitmotif* which reflected and encompassed hopes and dreams as much as love and work songs did.

❀❀❀

Any discussion of America's fascination with outlaws must begin with the archetypal brigand Robin Hood. He was well-known in the seventeenth and eighteenth centuries as he is to present-day devotees of Douglas Fairbanks and Errol Flynn, and accounted for more than one hundred ballads found on this continent. His activities against the Sheriff of Nottingham and Prince John may have lost their political significance, but taking from the rich to give to the poor struck a particularly responsive chord with victims of Tudor and Stuart inequities. (In some Appalachian ballads, the hero's name was changed to Robber Hood.) Nor did his disdain for royal property go unappreciated by early settlers:

> I'm going," said Robin, "to kill a fat buck
> For me and my Merry Men all;
> And likewise a doe before that I go,
> Or else it will cost me a fall."
>
> "You'd best have a care," the forester said,
> "For these are His Majesty's deer."

The ballad of "Johnny Cock" attests to the peril of poaching. Despite his mother's warning that seven wardens lay in ambush, Johnny and his hounds capture a deer. In the ensuing battle Johnny is wounded, but he manages to kill all but one of the attackers. American versions follow the story closely, with just some minor changes in nomenclature, including "Linkhorn" for "Lincoln" (as in the Lincoln green cloth worn by English hunters).

Ireland's equivalent of Robin Hood was Willie Brennan, a highwayman who flourished in the eighteenth century. "Brennan on the Moor" tells us that he

never robbed a poor man upon the King's
Highway
But what he'd taken from the rich . . .
He always did divide it with a widow in
distress.

Maritime ballads did not fare very well once colonists
found homes inland. One that did survive was "The
Golden Vanity," telling of a cabin boy who volunteered
to sink a Spanish ship by boring a hole beneath the water-
line. He completed the mission and returned to his ship,
but drowned when the captain (sometimes identified as
Sir Walter Raleigh) reneged on his promise of a reward,
and refused even to haul the lad back on deck. As with
other ballads, the names were changed when "The Golden
Vanity" crossed the sea. The enemy was sometimes Spanish, sometimes Turkish, and the ship of the title became
the "Sweet Trinity," "Merry Golden Tree," or "Turkish
Shiveree."

The broadside, a single printed sheet which was the
forerunner of the newspaper, became a popular colonial
item. Speading matters of current interest, it often contained "criminal goodnights," purported confessions of
men and women about to be executed told in ballad forms.
The authenticity of these confessions was dubious inas-
much as the sheets were printed several days in advance
of the event in order to be ready on the day of execution
and sold to the spectators. "Goodnights" followed a formula: identification, contrition for the crime (usually
described in gory detail), and at the end, a heartfelt plea
for salvation in the next world. The infamous pirate Captain Kidd was the subject of a well-known "goodnight"

where the repetitions in each verse echoed the measured
tread to the gallows:

Oh my name is William Kidd, as I sailed,
    as I sailed,
Oh my name is William Kidd, as I sailed;
Oh my name is William Kidd, God's laws I did
    forbid,
And most wickedly I did, as I sailed.

Oh my parents taught me well, as I sailed,
    as I sailed,
Oh my parents taught me well, as I sailed;
Oh my parents taught me well, to shun the
    gates of hell,
But against them I rebelled, as I sailed.

Oh I murdered William Moore . . .
And I left him to his gore, not many leagues
    from shore . . .

And being cruel still . . .
My gunner I did kill, and his precious blood
    did spill . . .

To the execution dock I must go, I must go,
To the execution dock, while many thousands flock,
But I must bear the shock and must die,
    And must die.

Take a warning now from me, for I must die,
    for I must die,
Take a warning now from me, and shun bad company,
Lest you go to hell with me, for I must die.

A very popular eighteenth-century broadside, "The Flesh Lad," contained elements of "goodnights," the Robin Hood ethic, and a spirit of outlaw bravado (the reference in the third stanza is to Henry Fielding, author of *Tom Jones* and founder of the Bow Street Runners, England's first professional police force):

When I was eighteen I took a wife,
I loved her dearly as I loved my life;
And to maintain her both fine and gay,
I went a-robbing on the King's highway.

I never robbed any poor man yet,
I was never in any tradesman's debt;
But I robbed the lords and the ladies gay,
And carried home the gold to my love straightaway.

To Cupid's Garden I did away,
To Cupid's Garden for to see the play;
Lord Fielding's gang there did me pursue,
And I was taken by the cursèd crew.

My father cried, "Oh darling son,"
My mother she wept and cried, "I am undone";
My mother tore her white locks and cried,
"Oh in his cradle he should have died."

Oh, when I'm dead and in my grave,
A flashy funeral let me have;
Let none but bold robbers follow me,
Give them good broadswords and liberty.

May six pretty maidens bear up my pall,
And let them have white gloves and ribbons all,
That they may say when they speak the truth,
There goes a wild and a wicked youth.

Folks on the American frontier liked this ballad so much that, just as brigands in Hanoverian England divided their booty among themselves, frontiersmen divvied up its verses for their own songs. The first stanza became part of "Rake and A-Rambling Boy" ("Rich and A-Rambling Boy" in one variant, giving the song a gentleman burglar quality). The second was a precursor of the "Jesse James-Robin Hood" ballads, while the last two are found in both the cowboy song "Streets of Laredo" and the blues "St. James Infirmary." The fourth verse was appropriated for "Louisville Burglar," whose rollicking rhythm belies its "goodnight" recriminations:

> I saw my aged father a-pleading at the bar,
> I saw my aged mother dragging out her hair;
> Dragging out those old grey locks, the tears
>   were streaming down,
> She says, "My son, what have you done, to be
>   sentenced to Frankfort town?"
>
> To you who have your liberty, pray keep it while
>   you can,
> Don't walk about the streets at night or break the
>   laws of man;
> For if you do you surely will, you'll find
>   yourself like me,
> Serving out your twenty-one years in the state
>   penitentiary.

There's no contrition at all in "Wild Bill Jones," a celebration of youthful recklessness. While their womenfolk sang of lovers dying of heartbreak, frontiersmen sang:

> As I went out for to take a little walk,
> I met upon that Wild Bill Jones;

A-walkin' and a-talkin' with my Lulu girl,
I told him to leave her alone.

He said, "My age it is twenty-one,
Too old for to be controlled,"
I pulled my revolver from off my side
And destroyed that poor boy's soul. . . .

Well, it's pass around your long-necked bottle,
And we'll all go on a spree;
Today was the last of that Wild Bill Jones
And tomorrow'll be the last of me.

The Civil War added to America's repertoire of adventurer songs. The border states of Kansas, Missouri, and Tennessee were the stamping ground for a host of marauders, many of whom were members of Quantrell's Raiders. Leading his band to harass Union forces, Charles Quantrell laid seige to Lawrence, Kansas, to avenge many times over the murder of his brother. One version of "Charlie Quantrell," to the tune of "Brennan on the Moor," paints its subject as a rebel Robin Hood using almost the same language as "Brennan":

A brace of loaded pistols he carried both
   night and day,
Though he never robbed a poor man while out
   on the highway;
But what he'd taken from the rich like toffs
   and like best,
He always did divide it with the widows in distress.

Another version chronicles the Lawrence incident with greater accuracy:

All routing and shouting and giving the
     yell,
Like so many demons just raised up from Hell;
The boys they were drunken with powder and wine,
And came to burn Lawrence just over the line.

Appomattox meant little to these people, for when the band
split up, northern banks and railroads remained fair game
to its alumni—among them the Dalton boys, Belle Starr,
Cole Younger, and Frank and Jesse James.

Jesse James endured as a legend not only for his Robin
Hood "rob from the rich and give to the poor" reputation,
but also for the underhanded manner in which he was
slain. A member of his gang named Robert Ford, purport-
edly to avenge Jesse's treatment of one of his relatives,
offered to kill "Mr. Howard" (the name which Jesse had
adopted when he retired) in exchange for a pardon from
the governor of Missouri. When James turned his back on
Ford to adjust a picture, he was shot by this man whom
he believed he could trust. The best-known version of the
ballad is:

> Jesse James was a lad who killed many a man,
> He robbed the Glendale train;
> He robbed from the rich and gave to the poor,
> He'd a hand, a heart, and a brain.

Chorus: Poor Jesse had a wife to mourn for his life,
> Three children they were brave;
> But that dirty little coward that shot Mr.
>   Howard
> Laid poor Jesse in his grave.

> It was on a Saturday night, poor Jesse was at
>   home,
> Talking to his family brave;

Robert Ford came along like a thief in the
   night
And laid poor Jesse in his grave.

(*Chorus*)

It was Robert Ford, that dirty little coward,
I wonder how he does feel;
For he ate of Jesse's bread and slept in
   Jesse's bed,
And laid poor Jesse in his grave.

(*Chorus*)

This song it was made by Billy Gashade
As soon as the news did arrive;
He said there was no man with the law
   in his hand
Who could take Jesse James when alive.

Although history does not record the identity of Billy
Gashade, the last stanza appears in most of the variants,
no matter how dissimilar in theme and content. In this
version, the second verse is repeated as a chorus, which,
together with the ballad's internal rhymes, makes it a hard-
driving favorite of country singers.*

But were such rebels the paragons of social justice and
victims of social injustice that their legends contend they
were? The story and song of Billy the Kid helps answer
that question. William H. Bonney is depicted in "Billy the
Kid" as a gallant though misguided lad:

* As a footnote to the story, Ford received his pardon and fled
to Colorado, where he too was ambushed by someone he had
antagonized.

> There's many a man with a face fine and fair,
> Who starts out in life with a chance to be square;
> But just like poor Billy he wanders astray,
> And loses his life in the very same way.

"Poor Billy" indeed! Bonney killed his first victim when he was twelve, gunning down a man he claimed had insulted his mother. Other victims followed when he fought for both sides during the Lincoln County, New Mexico, range wars, and he turned outlaw when he believed that the territorial authorities had reneged on an amnesty promise. Bonney had killed one man for each of his twenty-one years when Sheriff Pat Garrett overtook and killed him. But the people of New Mexico knew Billy for what he really was, and their view was considerably at odds with the tenor of the song. They knew he would never approach anyone in a fair fight, and as the *New York World* declared in its account of the slaying (datelined Las Vegas, New Mexico): "His death is hailed with great joy throughout this section of the country, as he had sworn he would kill several prominent citizens. . . . The coroner's jury returned a verdict of justifiable homicide coupled with the statement that Pat Garrett deserved the thanks of the whole community for ridding the country of the desperado." But people seldom care for newspaper reports as much as they do for picturesque legends and ballads.

Among the handful of songs about "good guys," "Texas Rangers" is notable for its combination of Eastern musical style and Western story line, showing again how older tunes were used as musical settings for contemporary events. To a modal melody (originally recorded with voice and fiddle sounding in unison), it chronicles a bloody nine-hour battle against a tribe of Indians. Like so many other adventuring songs, "Texas Rangers" concludes with a warning to the faint-hearted:

> And now my song is ended, I guess I've
>   sung enough,
> The life of any Ranger you see is very tough,
> And if you have a mother that don't want you
>   to roam,
> I advise you by experience, you'd better stay
>   at home.

❀❀❀

The spread of railroads and rural dislocation following the Civil War created the phenomenon of the hobo. The hobo, that knight of the road, was both the creator and subject of hundreds of songs. Initial unemployment led to a life-style of lethargy, for when not talking his way out of a loitering charge or begging a dinner without having to chop wood, the hobo celebrated his hand-to-mouth, footloose existence. An 1883 hymn, "Hallelujah, 'Tis Done," was easily parodied as "Hallelujah I'm a bum/Hallelujah, bum again/So give us a handout/To revive us again." Few hobo songs do not include references to trains and to a way of life surrounding the right-of-way. "The Wabash Cannonball" concluded with these lines:

> Now here's to Boston Blackie, may his name
>   forever stand,
> And aways be remembered by the 'boes throughout
>   the land;
> His earthly days are over and the curtains
>   'round him fall,
> We'll carry him home to victory on the Wabash
>   Cannonball.

The estimate that there were sixty thousand such wanderers during the 1880's led railroad officials to order a crackdown on the free rides permitted by brakemen. The hobo's life changed:

> The train was almost started,
> The conductor came by with his lamp;
> And whispered to me so kindly,
> "There's no room here for a tramp."

"Danville Girl" (also known as "Around a Western Watertank") more graphically described the realities of bumming around the country. Vermin-infested hobo jungles, association with vicious, bitter men, and the uncertainty of where the next meal was coming from turned hoboes' thoughts to what were once familiar sanctuaries:

> Around a western watertank, a-waiting for a
>   train,
> A thousand miles away from home, a-sleeping
>   in the rain;
> I walked up to the brakeman and gave him a line
>   of talk,
> He said, "if you've got money, I'll see that you
>   don't walk."
> "I haven't got a nickel, not a penny can I show."
> "Get off, get off, you railroad bum" and he slammed
>   the boxcar door. . . .
>
> Standing on the platform, smoking a cheap cigar,
> A-listening for the next freight train to catch
>   an empty car;
> My pocketbook was empty, my heart was full of pain,
> A thousand miles away from home, a-bumming a
>   railroad train.

The title "Man of Constant Sorrow" evokes Cervantes's epithet "Knight of the Woeful Countenance," but there is nothing at all quixotic about this Appalachian ballad's utter loneliness and total passivity:

> I am a man of constant sorrow,
> I have seen trouble all my days;
> I bade farewell to old Kentucky,
> The place where I was born and raised.
>
> For six long years I've been in trouble,
> My pleasure here on earth is done;
> For in this world I have to ramble,
> I have no friends to help me now.
>
> Oh, fare thee well, my own true lover,
> I fear I'll never see you again;
> For I am bound to ride that northern railroad,
> Perhaps I'll die upon the train.

Hoboing has almost completely disappeared, leaving just "Weary Willie" clown costumes, but the spirit (or dispiritedness) of rambling still remains in contemporary country music in a song like "King of the Road."

❀❀❀

Gambling was a profession which frequently led to instant mobility, especially after verbal dexterity failed to explain the appearance of a fifth ace. It was a life of traveling, so that any woman attracted by a suave, worldly-wise hustler had better know the stakes:

> I am a roving gambler, I gamble all around,
> Wherever I meet with a deck of cards I lay
> my money down....

Lay my money down, lay my money down,
Wherever I meet with a deck of cards, I lay
    my money down.

I had not been in 'Frisco many more weeks than
    three,
When I fell in love with a pretty little girl and
    she fell in love with me.

"Oh daughter, oh dear daughter, how can you treat
    me so,
And leave your aged mother and with the
    gambler go"

"Oh mother, oh dear mother, I'll do the best I can
If you ever see me coming back it'll be with the
    gambling man."

An optimistic philosophy was essential to boost morale
during losing streaks. For every "Jack O'Diamonds, I
knowed you of old; you have robbed all my pockets of
silver and gold," there was a "Don't let your deal go down,
till your last gold dollar is gone."

When bad cards and cold dice led to hot tempers, there
was blood on the pasteboards and bones. If John Henry's
fame rested on his dedication to an honest day's labor, not
so for another black with a similar name. According to
1891 West Virginia court records, John Hardy was con-
victed for killing a man in a crap game. The story became
a ballad in the "goodnight" style:

John Hardy was a desperate little man,
He carried a razor every day;
He killed a man on the West Virginia line,
You oughta seen John Hardy gettin' away,
    Poor boy, you oughta seen John Hardy getting away.

He ran till he came to the free state line,
And there he thought he'd be free;
But along came the sheriff and took him by the
    arm,
Said, "Johnny boy, you'd better come with me."

He sent for his momma and poppa too,
To come and go his bail;
But there ain't no bail on a murdering charge,
So they threw John Hardy back in jail.

"I've been to the East and been to the West,
Traveled this wide world around;
Been to the river and been baptized,
And now I'm on my hanging ground."

Another dice session was fatal for one Billy De Lyons
when he tangled with Richard Lee, a stacker on Mississippi riverboats:

I remember last September, 'twas on a Saturday
    night,
Stackolee and Billy De Lyons had a great fight.
He's a bad man, that cruel Stackolee.

Bill he shot six bits, Stack he bet he'd pass,
Stack pulled out his .45, said "You done shot
    your last."
He's a bad man, that cruel Stackolee.

Some versions turn Stackolee into a superman who, when
finally executed and consigned to the underworld, an-
nounces to Satan, "Stand back, Tom Devil, I'm gonna rule
Hell by myself." One variant concludes with the sangui-
nary:

Down in New Orleans there's a place called
   Lyons Club,
'Cause every step you step you're stepping in
   Billy De Lyons' blood.

❀❀❀❀

They call it that good ol' mountain dew,
And thems that refuse it are few;
Gonna hush up my mug if you fill up my jug,
With that good ol' mountain dew.

The risks of bootlegging, for years popular as an avoca-
tion and, occasionally, a livelihood, have been told and
retold in many a ballad. Even before federal troops were
sent to quell the 1794 Whiskey Rebellion, a segment of
rural society viewed government restrictions on the manu-
facture and sale of homemade alcohol as an affront to free
enterprise. They ran sour mash through tubing and con-
densers to yield home brew such as moonshine, white
lightning, or mountain dew. But they had to keep an eye
out for Treasury Department agents prowling hills and
hollows searching for their clandestine operations:

Wake up, wake up, Darlin' Cory,
What makes you sleep so sound?
The revenue officers are coming,
Gonna tear your still house down.

Avoiding detection required more than a little ingenuity. A West Virginian remembers: "Nine revenuers were
split up in three bunches. Work in the woods, lookin' for
stills. They'd put down a marker. It was my job to switch
the markers. And they'd get all confused. Everybody boot-

legged. It kind of got to be a legitimate business. You had to be foxier than the foxes, that's all."*

There were more fun and games when it came time to deliver the finished load. Specially adapted autos—with tanks in their trunks and souped-up engines—raced over hairpin mountain turns and through roadblocks, often only a few car lengths ahead of pursuing agents. It was an extraordinary baptism under fire for someone learning to double-clutch and power-spin around corners, and not a few drivers legitimized their ridge-running skills as amateur and professional stock-car racers.

There is still a breed of Southerner who considers running off a gallon or two an easy way to supplement his income. Prices have increased and penalties remain, but there will always be a market for home brew. As a good ol' boy from Tennessee took a slug from a Mason jar, he reflected, "That tax stamp just takes away the good taste." Seven hundred years ago he might have made a similar comment about a haunch of venison from one of the King's deer. Poaching and moonshining were caused by the same motives, and one man's meat became his descendant's potion. And what could be more revealing than the line in "Okie from Muskogee" that proclaims "white lightning's still the biggest thrill of all"?

❀❀❀

Fewer singers have had a greater desire for mobility but less of an opportunity than prisoners. With their days for

* From *Hard Times: An Oral History of the Great Depression,* by Studs Terkel. Copyright © 1970 by Studs Terkel. Published by Pantheon Books/A Division of Random House, Inc. Used by permission.

adventuring suspended, their thoughts naturally turned to freedom. The work songs of black convicts on road gangs and turpentine crews reflect this preoccupation:

> Says, "Come on gal
> And shut that door,"
> Says, "The dogs is comin'
> And I've got to go.
> Well-a two, three minutes
> Let me catch my wind,
> In-a two, three minutes
> Let me catch my wind,
> In-a two, three minutes
> I'm gone again."
>
> It's-a Long John,
> He's long gone.
> Like a turkey through the corn
> With his new clothes on,
> He's long gone.

Notions of actual escape were discouraged by the constant presence of guards and their vicious hounds:

> Well, I broke out of my cell when the jailer
>   turned his back, (twice)
> But now I'm so sorry, bloodhounds is on my track.
>
> Bloodhounds, bloodhounds, bloodhounds is on my
>   trail, (twice)
> They want to take me back to that cold, cold
>   lonesome jail.

The country classic "The Prisoner's Song" entertains a more wistful flight of fancy: "If I had the wings of an angel/Over these walls I would fly." Convicts found more down-to-earth metaphors in railroads, the "Midnight Special" 's and other trains which marked in counterpoint the boredom of a twenty-to-life stretch.

Unsuccessful escape attempts, brutality, and boredom made inmates think back to the security of their childhood. The lyrics of their songs, whether or not they were merely following time-honored conventions of "criminal goodnights," reflected sadness for lives misspent despite the good counsel of family and friends:

> If I had listened to what my mamma said,
> I wouldn't be here today;
> Laying around this old jail cell,
> Just weeping my poor life away.

❀❀❀

If anyone stands as the contemporary "adventurer," as this chapter describes that tradition, he would be Johnny Cash. In a somber frock coat and ruffled shirt, he seems to be equal parts rural circuit preacher belting out a sermon, riverboat gambler triumphantly filling an inside straight, and repentant prisoner. Cash was born in 1932 into a poor farming family in Arkansas. His emergence as a musician came in his mid-twenties when he joined with two others and gained a contract with Sun Records. (His first hit, "Hey Porter," told of a man eager to return to the South.) Switching to Columbia Records in 1958, Cash recorded "Don't Take Your Guns to Town," which might have been Wild Bill Jones's mother's advice to her impulsive son.

A growing reliance on drugs in the early 1960's almost proved to be Cash's professional and personal downfall.

He overcame the problem, however, and married June Carter, daughter of Mother Maybelle of the Carter Family (as close as country music could come to having a royal family). Cash achieved national prominence when he recorded an album live at Folsom Prison, California. With its time-honored metaphor of the freedom of railroads, his "Folsom Prison Blues" spoke for all inmates:

> Hear that train a'comin',
> It's rollin' 'round the bend,
> And I ain't seen the sunshine
> Since I don't know when;
> And I'm stuck in Folsom Prison,
> And time keeps draggin' on.*

Cash's continued popularity comes as much from his attitudes as from his musical talents. An early advocate of Indian and prisoner rights, Cash became involved with socially active popular singers. His repertoire includes a wide range of material, from songs by Bob Dylan and Kris Kristofferson to the traditional "Orange Blossom Special."

❀❀❀

The banjo was the first instrument to challenge the fiddle's exclusivity as *the* rural instrument. Himself something of a picker, Thomas Jefferson reported that the four-stringed "banjar," whose body was a hoof over which a piece of hide had been stretched, was most popular among slaves. A man named Joel Sweeney is credited with having

---

added, in the 1830's, a fifth string placed midway on the neck. The banjo's unchanging drone reminded mountain people of their ancestors' bagpipes, and with the fifth string, it lent itself to playing fiddle airs. Frets were placed across the neck to provide a more accurate and percussive sound. Two styles of playing predominated. Frailing (or "clawhammer," "beating" or "knockdown") used the index finger nail and thumb for a three-beat rhythm. "Double-thumbing" alternated picking between the four fretted and the fifth strings. A variety of tunings enabled the banjo-player to duplicate the fiddle's modal sounds. Although the five-stringed banjo enjoyed a vogue during the nineteenth century, it fell into disuse when its tenor cousin was chosen for jazz and dance band rhythm sections.

Mention country and western instruments and the guitar first comes to mind. It was not until the present century, however, that its use became widespread outside of cities, mainly via mail-order catalogues. Early rural playing pointed up the differences in technique between the white man's and the black man's music. The former simply played chords as accompaniment for voice or fiddle, whereas the latter treated the guitar as another voice, even as a chorus. They picked out melodies on one or more treble strings while keeping the beat with bass runs. As on the banjo, the left hand not only fretted chords but produced "blues notes" by stretching and sliding on the strings. (Slides also were made by fretting with a knife blade or bottle neck.) Played high on the guitar neck, such effects came close to sounding like an answering human voice.

There were other instruments too that spread from the

cities to the country. The mandolin neither looked nor was played like its Italian forebear. Country musicians found it easier to hold a flat-back model then the older gourd shape, and they picked with more pronounced, strident accents. The autoharp, a push-button zither, produced ethereal chords to match high-pitched mountain singing.

Rural musicians not only sang about moving around, they did it. Traveling through cities and towns after the Civil War, they demonstrated their own musical backgrounds and preferences to various audiences and discovered on their journey many others, some similar, some quite different. Whether returning home or continuing their trip, they shared what they had learned with new and old friends and neighbors, for if what they had heard pleased them, it went into the country kettle; they had never been sticklers for the kind of purity sought by folk song scholars.

Appalachian and delta musicians who headed toward the Southwest discovered that people rooted in other cultures were using many of the same instruments but played them in different styles. They heard Cajun music in Louisiana's isolated bayous and swamps. A corruption of "Arcadian," Cajun describes the descendants of the French settlers, driven from that Canadian province after Queen Anne's War, who found homes along the Gulf of Mexico (Longfellow's "Evangeline" chronicles their migration). High-school French is less than useful in deciphering Cajun patois. Based on waltzes and two-steps, Cajun music is characterized by insistant, accented fiddling backed by accordions and guitars, and exuberant yelps and mournful cries that recall aspects of plantation singing. Further on into Texas and the Southwest lay Mexican music, which was already an important influence on cowboy singing and playing. Its polished harmonies and mellifluous rhythms were more relaxed than those of Anglo-American ballads, yet more formally structured than black music.

Blacks who moved to New Orleans, Saint Louis and other Mississippi River cities learned to play saxophones, trumpets, and other unfamiliar instruments the way they had played banjos, fiddles, and drums—plantation style. Newcomers were fascinated by the range and interplay of dance bands performing the latest popular marches, schottisches and quadrilles. The piano, they found to their delight, could serve as an entire orchestra. Steady bass runs supported the right hand's syncopated improvisations within the traditional blues' I-IV-V chord progression or the circle of fifths (E to A to D to G to C—as in, more or less, "Sweet Georgia Brown") or any other progression that struck their fancy. Another chordal series from this era that was adopted by bluesmen and jazzmen is the tonic/dominant-of-relative-minor/subdominant/dominant (such as C-E7-F-G, as in the tune known to generations of guitar pickers as "Railroad Bill").

Whereas polite white society had accepted and enjoyed the music of antebellum minstrel shows, they disparaged the ragtime music which came from the sporting houses in the seamier sections of town. But its infectious mood was hard to resist and it soon became widespread. Blacks formed their own bands, and when trumpets, clarinets and trombones played contrapuntal solo-and-support melodies against piano, banjo, and drums, someone called it Dixieland. Harmonicas, washboards, and jugs were comman-

deered into jug bands. And when whites finally admitted
their interest and enthusiasm, black urban music became
more than just a footnote in the history of jazz.

As former slaves and their children moved through
Tennessee, Kentucky, the Carolinas, and Virginia, they
left an influence on white rural music. Country folks, on
hearing the inventiveness of this "new" music, had to
admit that there was more to it than merely scraping out
unadorned melodies on fiddles and plunking chords on
banjos and guitars. As in Irish and Negro railroad crews,
the two cultures could meet on common ground. Southern
towns held outings where white audiences sat facing one
side of the stage and blacks the other, and performers of
both races alternated in entertaining everyone. Moun-
taineers in the audiences were struck by the blues' three-
chord form, which they learned to fit to their own lyrics
and tonalities. They were excited by black guitar and
banjo techniques as well; the term "nigger-picking" which
they coined to describe this style of playing, was far from
pejorative. The most important white performers freely
acknowledged their debt to black itinerant musicians. The
Carter Family traveled throughout the South collecting
songs in the company of a black man named Leslie Rid-
dles, whose job was to memorize melodies. Mother Maybelle Carter herself fused black and white styles by picking out tunes on her guitar's bass strings while strumming
chords on the top three. Merle Travis's distinctive sound
is based on "choking" the strings—damping them while
finger-picking in blues syncopation. Dock Boggs, a renowned banjo player of the 1930's, claimed that he owed
his technique to "colored men who picked the banjo with

one finger and thumb. . . . I said to myself, never telling anyone, that was the way I was going to learn."*

The electronic age following World War I brought many changes to rural music. Phonographs, then radios, provided commercial outlets for country musicians beyond appearances in traveling medicine shows. Not only did these media offer a market for traditional ballads, but they exposed isolated communities to the wide range of recorded music available from other parts of the country and the world. Just as wanderers sometimes returned home to regale kinfolk with songs from the cities, popular songs heard over gramophones and wireless were adapted by rural musicians in ways that would have surprised their Tin Pan Alley composers. Perhaps the most exotic came from touring bands of Hawaiian Islanders. The whine of their steel guitars was a familiar sound to people who grew up on sliding whining fiddles. The steel guitar, also known as pedal steel, was outfitted with electronic devices to sustain notes and alter their pitch, and became a special feature in Western swing. That brand of country music developed in post-Depression Texas and Oklahoma, primarily through the efforts of Bob Wills. A fiddler and singer, Wills was a member of W. Lee "Pappy" O'Daniels's "Light Crust Doughboys," and, later, his own "Texas

---

* The place of blacks in contemporary country music requires just a footnote. Unlike many integrated string bands of the past, there are no black members of major country and western groups and there is only one featured artist who is black (though he sounds as if he's white). Country blues moved to cities and became the foundation for urban-based rock 'n' roll. It has now been refined into "soul," almost exclusively performed by blacks. Violins and electric organs have replaced fiddles and ragtime pianos, but links with the past include gospel-like harmonies while, of course, the beat goes on.

Playboys." Western swing music was dance music: a solid percussive beat, single or double fiddling, pedal steel, and often a brass section with saxophones, trumpets, and trombones. The Playboys' sound was jazzy, infectious, and above all entertaining, characterized by Wills's exhortations "Ah, play it Leon" and "now, isn't that purty!" to his musicians. The repertoire was extraordinarily varied, from traditional Appalachian tunes like "Cotton-Eyed Joe" and " 'Taters in the Sandy Ground," popular non-country songs such as "Caravan," to perhaps the best-known of the Playboys' Western swing-sound numbers, "Steel Guitar Rag" and "San Antonio Rose."

These were the elements of modern country and western music: the whiney, twangy sounds of "Hillbilly" songs. People from the South and Southwest liked it because, primarily, it was their music, a combination of vocal and instrumental styles not very different from their parents' and grandparents' music. It also came to represent country folk for urban dwellers who looked down their noses at any "rube" who came to town in his step-in overalls, with a piece of straw still hanging from his mouth. "Hayseed" and "hillbilly" were the epithets most frequently applied, and city dwellers chose to link the "hokey" sounds of rural music with the caricatures of country people. It was a way to try to assert one's superiority during the Depression era when many people needed desperately to find some sort of order amid the economic chaos.

One of the earliest yet most enduring outlets of country music began with the electronic era, via radio. Just as phonograph record producers scoured the hills for talent, radio programs were established during the 1920's to provide entertainment for residents of isolated communities as well as cities. The granddaddy of all such shows is Grand Ole Opry, inaugurated in 1925 and still a permanent fixture. It is a series of shows performed live on Friday and Saturday evenings from the Ryman Auditorium, a converted tabernacle church in downtown Nashville (replaced in 1974 by a new building in an amusement park called "Opryland"). The institution (for it is just that) is surrounded by a mystique rivaling that of the Metropolitan Opera, La Scala or vaudeville's Palace Theater. Knowing full well the value of an Opry appearance, performers pass up more lucrative engagements to sing only two or three songs at Opry. For their part, crowds lined up early in the day to insure places on the wooden pews lining the Ryman Auditorium's interior. Show time is a procession of established artists and rising stars shunted on and off the stage, while the audience reaction goes from mute adoration to foot-stomping, rebel-yelling exuberance. It is at Opry that one can see the real panorama of country and western music. Here the performers woo the audience as if their existence depended on it; they're at the Mother Church and they know it. A group playing the latest rock hit at full amplification may precede Bill Monroe, or Roy Acuff, who will finish his act by balancing his fiddle bow on his chin or doing yo-yo tricks. A toothsome girl in hotpants will be singing as flashbulbs pop, after which petticoated and string-tied clog dancers will tap out a fiddle hoedown. Millions more listen to these shows over WSM, hearing their favorite singers and instrumentalists sandwiched in between commercials for clothing, foodstuff, and record shops.

Several other country music programs have long been popular in their old locales via radio (and now television), including Cincinnati's Midwestern Hayride and the WWVA Jamboree ("50,000 powerful watts from Wheeling, West Virginia"). A common thread linking these shows is the spirit of from-studio-to-living-room. Emcees and artists strive to lessen the distance between microphone and radio set, as if neighbors had dropped by to visit and play on rural back porches. And the continuing popularity and longevity of Oprys, Hayrides, and Jamborees attest to the technique's success.

❀❀❀

Despite all that gallivanting around the country, there were still enough residents of Appalachian hills and hollows to make the region ring with songs and ballads dating back to colonial days, performed primarily for home entertainment. Then recording companies brought string bands (combinations of banjos, fiddles, guitars, mouth harps, and bass fiddles) in front of their microphones—groups with names to rival modern rock ensembles (Dr. Smith's Champion Horse Hair Pullers, the Aristocratic Pigs, the Skillet Lickers) and who played in a rough-hewn style. Then, in the 1940's, one man emerged with a different kind of string band music. It was Bill Monroe, "Father of Bluegrass."

Monroe widened the scope of string band music, adding elements of rhythms and harmonies that he learned from itinerant black musicians in his home state of Kentucky. While retaining Appalachian vocal techniques, Monroe devised a distinctive "potato bug" mandolin style with sharp accents and sliding glissandi. Then, in 1945, a five-string banjo player named Earl Scruggs joined Monroe's

Blue Grass Boys to set the standard for the type of music that later came to be known generally as bluegrass. Scruggs had devised a picking technique based on older two-finger styles, but refining them to produce melodies that stood out amid a cascade of grace notes. Coupled with hammering-on and pulling-off played by the left hand, Scrugg's three-finger picking technique turned the banjo into a lead instrument. The other instruments in Monroe's group became standard for this type of music as well: Fiddles, guitar, and bass fiddle accompanied the tenor lead backed by close trio or quartet harmonies. The result was a refinement of old-time string band music and something of a Southern rural amalgam—Appalachian modalities and instrumentation blended with blues' syncopation. Other string bands sought to cash in on the public's delighted response to The Blue Grass Boys, and when the Stanley Brothers recorded Monroe's "Molly and Tenbrooks," bluegrass became the name not just of a group but of a sound.

Scruggs left Monroe's group in 1948, and together with another Blue Grass Boys' alumnus, singer-guitarist Lester Flatt, he formed The Foggy Mountain Boys. They replaced the mandolin with an unamplified steel guitar called a Dobro, an instrument featured in several other bluegrass groups. The Foggy Mountain Boys performed at urban colleges and concert halls, all the while maintaining ties with rural fans, as described in the following description of a Grand Ole Opry appearance by novelist William Price Fox:

Flatt and Scruggs and the Foggy Mountain Boys came on like race horses, steel sharp and as right as railroad spikes. Spider smiled and jiggled his fingers and toes, tasting it as the music came right at him, tinny, whanging, wild. The high-pitched banjo crawled up on top, the low fiddle growl held at the side, while the steady driving Dobro underneath pushed it all together and straight out at him. It curled and skipped, danced and broke and raced forward, ricocheting off sheet metal onto some wilder level where heat lightning flashed and forked and waited. The Foggy Mountain Boys held the frenzied bridge for twenty-four straight bars, and Earl Scruggs tipped his white hat and stepped in tight. The rest backed. He came on somber-faced, expressionless, placid, and picking like a madman. High, shrill, and quick as a lizard. His jaw was set and his eyes were riveted to the twin spider hands as his ten fingers with twenty different things to do walked back and forth on the ebony-black and mother-of-pearl five-string frets. He went to the top of where he was going, held it, and then slid down in a machine-gun shower of sharp C, G, and A notes that moved like a ribbon and streaked out over the crowd to be heard a country mile away. He bowed quickly and stepped back as Lester Flatt, his guitar up high with the box to his ear, moved in. He sang with his eyes closed, his head cocked for range, and threw out his nasal, perfect tones in a short sowbelly arc that rose and fell, gathering in all the mountain folds, wood smoke, and purple twilights of the Cumberland Mountains. He was unconscious of the crowd, the back-up men, of himself. He heard only the music which raised him on his toes and twisted him around until his jaw was pointing to the back of the long curved hall. No one in the crowd spoke, coughed, or shifted. They strained forward, not wanting to miss a beat, a sound, a flash. The cameramen slid back, waiting for the song to end. It was an old song, "I Still Think the Good Things Outweigh the Bad." It wasn't gospel but it was close, and as the words hung in the heat and the hundred-year-old oak of Old Ryman it was gospel for Flatt. The back-up men moved in to pick him up. They were dark-eyed and haunted under their big shadow-throwing hats. Too many years and nights on the road had ground them down, but it had sharpened them and their music into the close-grained group they were. They heard each other and listened. They blocked for one another and dovetailed in right, building, breaking, and backing up with tight, close counterpoints. The fiddle player swooped in with wild slides and dips, stops, double stops and high, close, screech work at the top of the neck. They peaked and held, and then, easing off, they stepped aside as Mr. Earl Scruggs moved back in. He cranked the D tuner down, then up, on the peg head and slicing into a fresh key brought the house down with his blinding, showering finish.

The crowd rose shouting, whistling, rebel-yelling, and the flash bulbs exploded from everywhere.*

Meanwhile Bill Monroe continued as one of the premiere performers at Opry. A procession of talented pickers and singers served apprenticeships in The Blue Grass Boys, many going on to form their own bands, including Don Reno, Jimmy Martin, and Mac Wiseman. Others, such as Carter and Ralph Stanley and Jim and Jesse McReynolds, were heavily influenced by Monroe's style. These people drew upon their rural heritage for fiddle and banjo breakdowns like "Cripple Creek" and "Old Joe Clark," as well as sentimental ballads and spirituals. Bluegrass musicians wrote their own compositions to display fiddle, mandolin, and banjo virtuosity (a well-known example is "Foggy Mountain Breakdown," which was used as theme music for

Bonnie and Clyde) and, like other country musicians, played popular songs from the cities.

The folk explosion of the 1950's and 1960's included an upsurge of interest in bluegrass. A generation of urban fledgling banjo pickers played Scruggs's records at slow speeds to learn how to duplicate all the notes, while music stores and pawn shops did a brisk trade in mandolins and violins. City and country folk came together to share their mutual interest in the Dixieland-like solos and interplay polyphony of bluegrass.

❀❀❀

The adventuring tradition of country music's lyrics has been maintained only to a limited degree. Television, radio, and newspapers now make current events readily known, so that the broadside ballad is as unnecessary today as a chronicle. Perhaps the immediacy of these news media has made us realize that characters and situations that were formerly considered Romantic are in fact the products of social and psychological deviant behavior. Unlike the ballads about the assassinations of Garfield and McKinley, there have been no country songs about Sirhan, Oswald, or James Earl Ray. (A musical defense of My Lai's Lieutanant Calley, however, enjoyed a brief success.) Nor does one hear songs about recent murders or bank robberies, although the film *Bonnie and Clyde* included an appropriate bluegrass theme to capture the reckless glee with which those outlaws went about their business. Most adventure songs now come from Hollywood. "Thunder Road" was the title ballad of a movie about moonshining, while the Western flavor of the song

"High Noon" complemented the suspense of that Academy Award-winning film. Of this smattering of current songs, two echo older narratives. "Don't Take Your Guns To Town" is about the death of a youth who failed to heed his mother's advice. "El Paso," with a Mexican-sounding melody, evokes elements of "Wild Bill Jones" and Western relentlessness. After the singer shoots down a rival who had made overtures to his girlfriend, he flees to New Mexico. Finding that his love for the maiden is stronger than his fear of death, he returns to El Paso, where he is mortally wounded in an ambush and dies in his beloved's arms.

Mobility, however, has kept its place at the heart of country music, whether or not told in terms of occupations. Audiences enjoy both old and new songs about the comings and goings of anonymous country heroes. Some set off by foot:

> I got the keys to the highway, still I'm bound
>   to go,
> Gonna leave here running, 'cause walking's way
>   too slow.

Others by railroad:

> That big eight wheeler rollin' down the track
> Means your true lovin' Daddy ain't comin' back,
> I'm movin' on.*

Or by ship:

> I wish I was in London or some other seaport town,
> I'd set my feet on a steamboat and sail the ocean
>   'round.

* From the song I'M MOVIN' ON. Copyright 1950 by Hill and Range Songs, Inc. Used by permission.

The joys of wandering described in "King of the Road" seem to be the exception; most of the lyrics reveal that the adventurer is nothing more than a peripatetic loser:

> White line fever,
> A sickness born down deep within my soul;
> White line fever,
> The years keep flyin' by like the high line poles.*

Country boys find cities cold, unappealing, and full of strange folkways:

> It ain't nothing but a concrete jungle
> With people packed like sardines,
> Where everybody's tryin' to live beyond their means.
> Where all the natives hurry and scurry to and fro,
> And like fleas on a puppy dog they got no place
>   to go.
> I wouldn't live in New York City
> If they gave me the whole dang town.†

People from Kentucky, Tennessee, and Missouri who have moved to Detroit, Chicago, and Cleveland congregate in taverns where the jukebox is strictly country. These "adventurers"—lonely, tired, and poor—listen to old songs like:

> I wonder how the old folks are at home,
> I wonder if they miss me while I roam.

---

* From the song WHITE LINE FEVER, words and music by Merle Haggard. Copyright ©1969 Blue Book Music. Used by permission.

† From the song I WOULDN'T LIVE IN NEW YORK CITY. Words and music by Buck Owens. Copyright ©1970 Blue Book Music. Used by permission.

I wonder if they pray
For the boy who went away,
And left his dear old parents all alone.

That farm might have been a hovel as poor as Job's turkey,
and perhaps leaving was the best thing a lad could have
done, but be it every so humble . . .

4

Take Me Home

THE APPEAL OF COUNTRY MUSIC

Johnny Cash.
(Country Music Association)

The Carter Family.
(Country Music Association)

Bill Monroe. *(Country Music Association)*

A typical hillbilly string band on stage at Grand Ole Opry. *(Country Music Association)*

Earl Scruggs and Lester Flatt. *(Wide World Photos)*

Cars lined up bumper-to-bumper waiting to get into the fiddler's convention at Galax, Virginia. *(Photo Researchers)*

Kris Kristofferson.
(Country Music Association)

The Nitty Gritty Dirt Band.
(Country Music Association)

The music festival was into its second day and a stream of cars still waited to get onto the grounds, license plates forming a patchwork of colors. In spite of summer heat and humidity, windows had been rolled down and air conditioning turned off so that occupants could try to catch the strains of music that drifted their way. For those already on the grounds, the afternoon was a twenty-ring circus. Charcoal grills smouldered in the parking lot beside station wagons and campers. Most of the performers who were to appear in the evening's concert hung around their buses, signing autographs, selling records, or just catching up on gossip with members of other bands.

In a nearby field, where a stream cascaded into a waterfall, a group of people made music under a shade tree. A tall, balding man tapped his toe as he thumped bullfrog sounds out of a bass fiddle. The guitar player was a slim, tanned, college-age girl wearing cut-off jeans and an expensive-looking blouse. She was smiling at her boyfriend, who was stomping out a surrealistic buck-and-wing in the stream. The fiddler couldn't have been more than fourteen years old, his horn-rimmed glasses sliding over his nose while he played with the concentration of a watchmaker. The dude on banjo had all the trappings of an automobile commercial's Southern sheriff in civvies: straw porkpie hat, open-collared short-sleeved shirt, khaki trousers, white socks, and penny loafers. Without missing a beat, he was grinning and winking at the guitarist, until his wife appeared to jab him smartly in the ribs.

A man made his way through the group of listeners.

"Isn't that ——?" whispered someone. The bass player did a double take and nodded. He stepped back to permit the newcomer through. The man wore a ten-gallon hat, string tie, and fancy-tooled boots. He unslung a mandolin from over his shoulder and took a pick from his shirt pocket. As the fiddler took the melody part in the lively breakdown the group was playing, the professional accompanied with soaring harmonies, taking care not to overshadow his young colleague. Then he turned his attention to the banjo picker, who, finding himself playing along with the famous musician, began to miss notes and became more flustered with each mistake. The mandolin player led him through the tune again until it sounded right, then launched into a solo of his own. When the song was over, he shook hands with the group's members (with a courtly bow to the girl), autographed someone's program, and moved off across the field toward another cluster of players.

World War II did much to spread country music outside its native areas. Northerners attending boot camps in the South heard nothing but "hillbilly" over local radio stations, while almost every barracks and foxhole overseas had at least one GI who strummed along or just listened to it over the military networks. Those who might otherwise have considered themselves above its unsophisticated lyrics found that the words had special appeal to people of all backgrounds preoccupied with sweethearts back home and dreading the arrival of "Dear John" letters. The music also came to represent many of the institutions they were fighting to preserve, homely virtues represented by apple pie and motherhood. After countless hours of listening to country songs, many former soldiers and sailors later discovered that the sounds of a ballad by Hank Williams or Webb Pierce recalled memories of military service as much as a plate of chipped beef on toast.

Like the explosion of a motorcycle backfiring, rock'n'roll arrived on the scene in the mid-1950's. Once included in record catalogues as "rhythm and blues" or "Race" solely for black audiences, rock'n'roll, with its danceable beat and unabashed lyrics, rapidly became the folk music of the unsilent generation. Young people had grown tired of listening to Hit Parade songs concerned with pyramids along the Nile, old Cape Cod, and doggies in the window, which they considered antediluvian. Rock'n'roll spoke to their energies and interests. It was no accident that many Southerners became top performers in this field, fusing as they did elements of their heritage: "patting Juba" sensuality and exuberance, blues chords, gospel harmonies, and Western swing rhythms. Elvis Presley is a prime example of this blend. Growing up in rural Mississippi, he cut his musical eye teeth on church singing (he attributed his stage gyrations to his observation of the fervent tremors of revivalist preachers) and was influenced in his style by Ernest Tubb, Roy Acuff, and Jimmie Rodgers and bluesmen Muddy Waters and Howlin' Wolf. His first record epitomized this racial confluence: "That's All Right, Mama" and (on the flip side) Bill Monroe's bluegrass classic "Blue Moon of Kentucky". Some rural rockers never lost their country flavor. The Everly Brothers sang in close mountain harmonies like the older sibling duets of the Monroe and Louvin brothers; their father, Ike Everly, had been a highly regarded guitar player in string bands, and the Everlys acknowledged their debt to both him and Appalachian balladry in albums such as "Songs Our Daddy Taught Us."

Established country performers as well as urban pop stars learned that cash registers rang to the tune of teen-age purchasing power. Marty Robbins and Sonny James had nationwide hits with, respectively, "A White Sport Coat (And A Pink Carnation)" and "Young Love." Two non-rock but rural-based songs during this period were the mining complaint "Sixteen Tons" and "The Battle of New Orleans." The latter celebrated Andrew Jackson's victory in the War of 1812; fiddlers who recognized the .melody as the traditional "Eighth of January" must have alternately chuckled and jealously gnashed their teeth at the way old songs could continue to be made attractive to urban audiences.

The later years of the 1950's saw rock'n'roll share the spotlight with commercialized folk music. Groundwork had begun some twenty-five years before, when Burl Ives, Richard Dyer-Bennett, and Josh White entertained supper club patrons, while The Weavers and Woody Guthrie spun songs reflecting liberal political leanings (the Weavers, however, also had a Top Ten hit with "Goodnight Irene"). The folk boom began in earnest with the Kingston Trio's version of the North Carolina murder-for-love ballad "Tom Dooley." Some purists pointed with dismay at their "The M.T.A. Song," a parody of "The Wreck of the Old '97," either not knowing or caring that the older railroad ballad was itself based on "The Ship That Never Returned." Studied arrangements of rural love, work, and adventure songs were rampant, and Harry Belafonte, Peter, Paul and Mary, and The Brothers Four made college and concert hall tours. A consequence of this interest was that their audiences were moved to make music themselves. Just as the apathy of the "Eisenhower Generation" was followed by student involvement in political and social issues, so it became more important for youngsters to pick a guitar or banjo than merely to listen to others play. For some urban pickers and singers, rudimentary skills were not enough, so they scoured record shops for Library of Congress discs of authentic country music and albums made by Southern instrumentalists. As citybillies marveled at and mastered their techniques, they came to appreciate the attitudes expressed by the music and the life from which it came. It was Sherman's march all over again as Yankee young'uns armed with gold-plated $500 banjos entered (and sometimes won) Old Time Fiddlers and bluegrass competitions. Country musicians toured urban circuits, while aficionados from all over the country traveled to festivals at Newport, Rhode Island, and Monterey, California, which presented a wide range of American native music, ranging from then newcomers Joan Baez and Bob Dylan to rediscovered landmark figures such as Mississippi John Hurt.

Meanwhile, back in the studios the invasion of British pop groups in the 1960's marked the transition from rock-'n'roll to "hard rock," a term describing a class of music that uses harsher electronic sounds. Its appeal was sensory, analogous to hallucinogenic drugs then in vogue. The impact of rock on country music was indirect, in that performers raised in rather conservative rural ways had been willing to accept and participate in rock'n'roll— just good ol' boys letting off a little musical steam—but drew the line at rock's "pure noise" and the subculture it represented. But if they looked beyond the performers' long hair and the amplifiers' feedback, they would have learned that foreign groups like the Beatles and the Rolling Stones had their origins in the music of Chuck Berry, Fats Domino, Buddy Holly, and other rhythm and blues musicians. Such music struck British lads as exotic; in the words of Ian Whitcomb, "We had rockabilly without racism, and rhythm and blues without rednecks." The Rolling Stones played the blues tune "I'm a King Bee" and the heavily syncopated "Honky Tonk Woman," while the Animals recorded a version of the blues classic "House of the Rising Sun." Few who heard Traffic's "John Barleycorn Must Die" were aware of its origin as an English fertility ballad.

The Beatles' Ringo Starr has long been a great country music fan. He included country songs on almost every one of the group's records and then went on to make a solo album in Nashville. Its contents captured the core of lover-as-loser themes, including songs titled "Love Don't Last Long," "Fastest Growing Heartache in the West," "Loser's Lounge," and the name of the album, *Beaucoup of Blues*. The album came about when Ringo mentioned to a Nashville musician visiting England that he wanted to make a country album. "Come to Nashville," Ringo was told, "we can do it within a week." The session lasted two days, as it turned out, just another testimony to the professionalism of Music City's studio musicians.

❀❀❀

Partially in reaction to acid rock indigestion caused by unrelieved raucousness and frenetic renditions, folk-rock's understated melodies and harmonies and "down home" lyrics grew in popularity. Its exponents had grown up during the preceding decade's folk craze. They were as familiar with banjos and autoharps as with electric guitars and Fender basses. The most important figure in this area is Bob Dylan. Dylan first achieved acclaim for songs that reflected his generation's political and social involvement, delivered in a crude singing style evocative of his idol Woody Guthrie. After a flirtation with hard rock, his lyrics and music moved to the country, marked by the *Nashville Skyline* album. Dylan's compositions may be found in many country artists' repertoires. Johnny Cash was among the first to recognize Dylan's talents, having joined him in one song on the Nashville record. Flatt and Scruggs included Dylan's songs on several of their albums.

The progress of Joan Baez's repertoire is something of a history of country music in itself. She began by singing British ballads and their Appalachian descendants. The record she cut with The Greenbriar Boys early in her career was a precursor of recent albums cut in Nashville containing almost exclusively country and western material.

The rural elements of this music have now been given recognition by the term "country rock." Country rock performers play both contemporary and traditional material. The Flying Burrito Brothers sound as comfortable with a Merle Haggard tune as The Byrds (whence several Burrito Brothers came) with the traditional apostrophe to a hound dog named "Old Blue." The Canadian duet Ian and Sylvia added steel guitars and drums and called their new group "The Great Speckled Bird" after Roy Acuff's classic spiritual. The songs of Tim Hardin have a strong rural flavor, especially "If I Were a Carpenter" and the moving "Tribute to Hank Williams." The Band, Dylan's celebrated back-up group, has become successful in its own right for its ragtime, old-timey sound.

A more recent instance of youngsters joining old-timers resulted in the album *Will the Circle Be Unbroken*. Participants included Earl Scruggs, Doc Watson, Roy Acuff, Merle Travis, Jimmy Martin, and Mother Maybelle Carter, along with the Nitty Gritty Dirt Band, a folk-rock group which has gravitated to country music. Listening to Dirt bandsman John McEuen (playing a banjo once owned by Uncle Dave Macon) and Scruggs pick away at an arrangement of the old fiddle tune "Soldier's Joy," one is once again caught up by the familiarity and appreciation of country music to be found everywhere. Scruggs himself has branched out into more contemporary music. He and Lester Flatt parted company in 1969; Flatt remains involved in traditional bluegrass, while Scruggs joined sons Randy and Gary to play in a more modern fashion. They do, for example, the old tune "Reuben" with electric guitars, bass, piano, and drums accompanying Scrugg's five-string banjo.

Country musicians have welcomed these urban visitors into their down home tradition with typical Southern hospitality. There is another cross-cultural and -generational get-together on an album featuring two Appalachian pickers, Obray Ramsey and Byard Ray. In addition to their own banjo-fiddle duets, they are joined by Judy Collins, Eric Anderson, and others for contemporary country rock selections. Kris Kristofferson's country-influenced songs are often performed by more traditional country musicians such as Johnny Cash and Jerry Lee Lewis. Some Nashville cats may take issue with Joan Baez's political views, but they are quick to applaud her enthusiasm for and facility with their brand of music.

With respect to instrumentation and recording techniques, country music had not been very different from rock and other forms of popular music. In the early days of the phonograph, a string band was led into a studio, someone started the machine, and the fellers played until they were told to stop. Then, in the 1950's, the age of specialization and electronic gadgetry reared its tape head. Initially, electric guitars only increased the level of volume, but soon their amplifiers were resounding with tremolos, echo chambers, and vibrators. Steel guitars had been fitted with pedals to sustain notes and chords. Other, non-folk instruments were added: piano, played in the tinkly, "slip-note" style devised by Floyd Cramer; and, for further lushness, violins (as distinguished from fiddles), brass sections, and voice choirs singing background harmonies. The result was a more polished, "contemporary" sound.

The increased number of participants in the recording process has meant that musicians don't always see the artist whom they accompany. The singer records his part backed only by several guitars, piano, and rhythm section. The session's producer and engineer then "mix" the tapes (each instrument has been recorded on a separate track to allow volume adjustment). The product becomes the "solo" against which will be taped a string section to be added to the master tape. A vocal chorus may be the final element. Preparing a record in stages permits a producer to adjust components as he goes along without the problem (and cost) of redoing an entire session. If he feels something is lacking, he can add an instrument, section, or chorus, or even overdub the singer doing another vocal line in harmony with himself. Such electronic sleight of hand neither denigrates nor detracts from studio musicians' attitudes toward their work. Rather than feeling like cogs in a wheel, they take pride in their contributions to this step-by-step process.

Because of the great number of country albums being produced, songwriters seem to be working overtime. Although the dream of arriving in Nashville with a pocketful of tunes and being discovered overnight is an appealing one, it just doesn't happen these days. Performers either write their own material or work with professional tunesmiths who know their style and range. "Overnight successes," whether composers or performers, are people who have been in the business for many years. They may have washed dishes, worked as secretaries or sidemen, or done anything else to survive, while hanging around the fringes of the business trying to be heard. If they're lucky, a producer or A & R man will take notice and decide the time is right for a particular kind of sound or type of lyric. If he's correct, if the public agrees, it's gravy for everyone involved. Otherwise, it's back to grits for the musician or composer.

Since the days when it was used by medicine shows to sell snake oil elixir, country music has never lost its commercial value. Madison Avenue has associated it with things "natural" and "honest" in advertisements on national radio and television that proffer shampoo, beer, and fruit wine to down-homey jingles which emphasize the items' purity. Even a commercial for kosher wine has a bluegrass background. Business interests also exploit the country sound for its connotation of rugged independence.

"Bonnie and Clyde" banjo tunes help sell automobiles, while soft drink ads set to guitar and fiddle obbligatos invite us to break away to discover our "inner, truer selves." On regional levels, seed-and-feed stores continue to sponsor local radio shows that give farm prices and weather reports amid a hailstorm of country and western selections; while listeners to "Top Forty Country Hits" or "Gospel Ship" are invited to buy plastic Jesus figurines, a couple of dozen live baby chicks, and bail bonds.

Country music has also traveled across the seas. Two young Japanese visitors holding guitars and banjo cases stood diffidently outside a circle of bluegrass musicians one day in New York's Washington Square Park, the traditional gathering place of Greenwich Village folksingers. A verbal invitation to join in brought no response from the two foreigners, but gestures did. Whereupon the two fellows launched into a rendition of Bill Monroe's "Rawhide" that left their audience speechless. Neither boy spoke any English, but a translator explained what they liked about country music: "It's fun to make." The music's popularity abroad began with American forces stationed in Europe and Asia, transmitted through bars on and off the military bases. It is especially popular in Japan, where touring American artists draw large audiences. Native bluegrass groups there not only duplicate note-for-note and syllable-for-syllable the records of the Stanley Brothers, Reno and Smiley, and Flatt and Scruggs, but compose original songs which capture the spirit of hills considerably east of Mount Fuji. The British too have shown a tremendous interest in American rural music. Members of folk and old-time music clubs in London and other English cities pursue historiography and discographies with the zeal of doctoral candidates. Young people in the Soviet Union listen to recorded country music with greater impunity than rock albums brought in from the West, since Soviet cultural officials have given it something of an imprimatur for its noncapitalistic "worker" qualities.

One cannot listen to any form of modern jazz without noticing its rural music antecedents. As it developed in cities after World War I, it continued to blend the ragtime syncopation, church harmonies and vocal techniques common to plantation work songs. Much of the music during this period was set within a blues framework, as pianos, trumpets, and trombones (or some other combination) took the role of country guitars and banjos at the end of each line. Singers Bessie Smith and Billie Holiday and trumpeters Jelly Roll Morton and Louis Armstrong carried on the same stylistic liberties in their performances. Big bands replaced smaller combos and played stricter arrangements, but there was still room for solo improvisation.

Contemporary jazz has maintained these connections to its rural cousins. The hard bop playing of Charlie Mingus and Thelonious Monk sounds, in the jazz expression, "funky," with a back-to-the-roots earthiness. The free form and atonality of third-stream jazz may be further afield, but the yelps of Ornette Coleman's saxophone evoke the plaintiveness and outrage of a plantation worker's holler.

Rural melodies and rhythms have also been used by serious composers in vocal, instrumental, and ballet works. Just as John Gay took ballad tunes for *The Beggar's Opera* and Béla Bartók collected Hungarian folk material, both American and foreign musicians drew from the wellspring of this country's indigenous songs and dances. Kurt Weill incorporated several Appalachian ballads and banjo tunes into his folk opera *Down In The Valley*, including "Lonesome Dove," "Sourwood Mountain," and "Hop Up Ladies." George Gershwin used blues and ragtime tempos and tonalities in *Porgy and Bess*, especially flatted thirds and sevenths in "It Ain't Necessarily So."

Aaron Copland chose cowboy songs—"Goodbye Old Paint," "Get Along Little Dogie," and "The Dying Cowboy"—to provide horseback rhythms in his music for the ballet *Billy The Kid*. His suite *Appalachian Spring* contains the lovely Shaker hymn " 'Tis a Gift To Be Simple." Further examples of the orchestral use of rural music include Darius Milhaud's *Opus Americana*, Roy Harris's *Folk Song* Symphony, and Ralph Vaughan Williams's Variations on *Greensleeves*, the latter based on the famous English folk song.

Less well-known compositions, written by Southerners, include *From the Southern Mountain* by Lamar Stringfield, *Negro Folk Symphony #1* by William L. Dawson, and *Danse Louisianaise* by Christian Jordan. Ferde Grofe, whose "On The Trail" movement of *Grand Canyon* echoes the clip-clop of horses' hooves, was inspired by Cajun country bayous and swamps to write his *Mississippi* Suite.

❁❁❁

"Home" is the most prevalent theme in country and western music. Shattered romances, physical and spiritual fatigue, and geographic disorientation have caused yearnings for something stable, comfortable, and comforting; both literally and metaphorically, that place is home.

"Take Me Home" songs can be divided into three groupings, of which the first concerns returning to specific places. These songs range in subject matter from the hamlets of "Flat River, Missouri" and "Rocky Top, Tennessee" to cities such as "Galveston," "Louisville," and "Abilene" (songs in praise of urban areas are acceptable if (1) the cities are in the South, and (2) they provide fond memories). Every state below the Mason-Dixon line is celebrated in song: a representative listing would include "Carry Me Back To Old Virginny," "Carolina Mountain Home," "Alabama Bound," and "Georgia Pineywood." Paeans to the Bluegrass State might begin with "My Old Kentucky Home" and extend to "Kentucky Means Paradise" and "Just A Song Of Old Kentucky," while its neighbor to the south, the home of Davy Crockett, is represented by the breakdown "Tennessee." Some conventional, some imaginative, these lyrics show the pride and nostalgia for the place of one's birth and youth.

The second category is more abstract, something of an "abandon all hope" statement, as in "Man of Constant Sorrow," or:

> My home is across the Blue Ridge Mountains . . .
> And I never expect to see it anymore.

Echoing the title of Thomas Wolfe's (himself a product of North Carolina's hill country) book *You Can't Go Home Again* is the sad conclusion:

> You know it's hard to get back home,
> Where the grass is green and the sun is warm;
> Yeah, a home-cooked meal would sure taste good,
> And the night to spend with the ones you love.*

But try they will, for the simple reason that nostalgia for the comfortable and familiar is an inexorable force. The South, in its geography, customs, and family ties, provides a goal for the traveler; the South has been represented in song as a metaphor for home in ways unmatched by other regions of this country:

> I'm going to the station, gonna catch the fastest
>   train that goes;
> I'm going back South where the weather suits
>   my clothes.
>
> I was raised in the country, where the snow it
>   never fell;
> I'm going back South if I don't do so well.

In country music, the South, the country, and home have always shared an identity of interest. Bucolic scenes are recalled—"cattle lowing in the lane," fox hunting with one's father, flowers blooming in mountain pastures. A writer raised in the Southwest on Western swing music recalls in song how his family would pile into a car and drive for hours just to hear The Light Crust Dough Boys:

> Was in the town of Tulsa, 'bout thirty years ago,
> At Cain's Academy down in old Oklahom'.
> Well, the dust was blowin', but the music was right,
> And W. Lee O'Daniel played all night.*

Parents seem to prompt the fondest memories and strongest desires to return home. Their sadness at seeing their children leave the nest and their dire predictions about life's problems loom large in recollections of warmth and support. Despite Freudian excavations, home means "That Silver-Haired Daddy of Mine" and:

> Just a village and a homestead on the farm,
> And a mother's love so true.

Not only "old-timers" reminisce about the past and its halcyon days. Writers and performers of all ages choose "home" songs not only for their commercial durability but from honest feelings about their birthplaces. Just to scan any list of songs written during the past five years shows titles such as "Don't It Make You Want To Go Home," "Drivin' Home," "Homecoming," "Homesick," "I'm Going Home," "South," and one in particular which sold over one million copies on both country and "pop" charts, "Take Me Home, Country Roads":

> I hear her voice, in the morning light it calls me,
> Radio reminds me of my home far away;
> Driving down that road I get a feeling that I
>   should have been home yesterday ... yesterday.
>
> Country roads, take me home
> To the place I belong;
> West Virginia, Mountain Mama,
> Take me home, country roads.*

Its harmonies and chord changes may make the song musically more sophisticated than "Take Me Back To

---

* TAKE ME HOME, COUNTRY ROADS. Words and music by Bill Danoff, Taffy Nivert and John Denver. Copyright © 1971 by Cherry Lane Music Co. Used by permission. All Rights Reserved. International Copyright Secured.

The Sweet Sunny South," but its lyrics continue the same spirit as the older minstrel show and mountain ballad:

> Take me back to the place where I first saw
> the light,
> To the sweet sunny South take me home;
> Where the wild birds sing me to sleep every night,
> Oh why was I tempted to roam?

The enduring popularity of country music's "take me home" theme may lie in a combination of the metaphors of love, work, and adventure. People in love want to be with their loved ones, whether family or that one special reason. Home is where the heart is. People who work at certain occupations, particularly those associated with rural areas, make their living from natural elements, whether cottage industry or being close to the soil. The adventurer knew all about home, and we know that his lot was different from ours. He had a greater opportunity to succeed on his own, the results depending on how he used his wits and skills. Just as he was envious of people who could return home, so we, enmeshed in an overcrowded and highly technological world, envy the adventurer. Who would not agree with this statement of the contemporary human condition from James Jones's *From Here To Eternity?*

> Maybe back in the old days, back in the time of the pioneers, a man could do what he wanted to do in peace. But he had the woods then, he could go off and live alone. He could live well off the woods. And if they followed him for this or that, he could always just move on. There was always more woods ahead. But a man can't do that now. He's got to play ball with them. He has to divide it all by two.

Life seems to have become a treadmill, evoking Lewis Carroll's line about having to run twice as fast just to stay in the same place. Certainly settlers, migrants, and outlaws had no bed of roses, but they seemed, we think, to have had more options than we do.

Maybe we're getting smarter. Personnel departments now are forced to talk with prospective employees about "job satisfaction" when once salary was all that was discussed. Personal involvement has become an important criterion in work and in life, just as leisure time has become a more important part of our existence. An executive stranded on a stalled commuter train can't wait to get home to rake leaves or putter around his basement workbench. That truckdriver stuck in freeway traffic buoys his spirits with thoughts of weekend skimobiling. A schoolteacher muses during the week about a weekend at the seashore in bare feet and blue jeans. It's all part of an attempt to recapture control of our lives in direct and personal terms. Young people have seized on the process, looking for an optimism in the present as well as future. Communal experiences, casual clothing, and liberated lifestyles have become their hallmarks. And one place they find what they're looking for is in country music. People of all ages realize that in any escape from the complexities of contemporary society, there can be nothing more appealing than childhood memories. All roads, as American country music has always demonstrated, lead to home.

NOTES

Chapter 1

page 17 The history and social material described in this and succeeding chapters come primarily from Current, *A History of the United States* and Furnas, *The Americans*.

21 For striking examples of the bagpipes' influence on fiddle playing, listen to: "Scotland" (Ramsey and Ray: *White Lightning—Fresh Air*); "The Scotch Musick" (*Ballads and Breakdowns from the Southern Mountains*); and "June Apple" (Doc Watson: *Good Deal*). "Cumberland Gap" (Ramsey and Ray) and "Sally Goodin" (*Ballads and Breakdowns*) are two of the many letting-off-steam fiddle tunes.

22 The most complete (and formidable) collection of British ballads is *The English and Scottish Popular Ballads* (5 vols.) compiled by Child. *The Ballad of Tradition* offers synopses of the most common ballads together with literary and musical criticism. Richard Dyer-Bennett has recorded many ballads in freely arranged settings. (See the Discography for details on these and other record references in the notes.)

23 "Black Jack Davy" (Harry and Jeanie West: *New Lost City Ramblers*, vol. 4).

page 24   "Barbara Allen" (Jean Ritchie: *British Traditional Ballads in the Southern Mountains*, vol. 1; *Versions and Varients of "Barbara Allen"*).

25   "Lord Thomas and Fair Ellender" (*Anglo-American Ballads*).

27   "Little Matty Groves" (*Joan Baez*, vol. 1; Doc Watson: *Home Again*).

"The House Carpenter" (Joan Baez, vol. 1; *Ballads and Breakdowns from the Southern Mountains*).

28   "Georgie Collins" (*New Lost City Ramblers*, vol. 2; *Old Time Music at Clarence Ashley's*, vol. 2).

29   "The Lass of Loch Royale" (Paul Clayton: *Folk Ballads of the English-Speaking World; Ballads and Breakdowns from the Southern Mountains*).

"Pretty Little Miss" (*Country Music and Bluegrass at Newport—1963*; New Lost City Ramblers: *Gone to the Country*).

"Froggie Went A-Courtin'" (Doc Watson: *Home Again*).

30   "Single Girl" (*Anthology of American Folk Music*, vol. 3).

"I'll Be No Man's Wife" (Flatt and Scruggs: *Folk Songs of Our Land*).

"The Coo-coo Bird" (*New Lost City Ramblers*, vol. 4).

32   "Pretty Polly" (The Dillards: *Live—Almost*, with an amusing introduction; Dock Boggs: *The Legendary Dock Boggs*; Keith & Rooney: *Livin' On The Mountain*; Paul Clayton: *British and American Murder Ballads*).

"Naomi Wise" (*Old Time Music at Clarence Ashley's*, vol. 2).

"Poor Ellen Smith" (Flatt & Scruggs: *Folk Songs of Our Land; Ballads and Breakdowns from the Southern Mountains; The Country Gentlemen*).

"Banks of the Ohio" (*Joan Baez*, vol. 2; Earl Scruggs: *I Saw The Light*).

page 33   "Tom Dula" (*New Lost City Ramblers,* vol. 2).
           "Rose Connolly" (Paul Clayton: *British and Amer-
           ican Murder Ballads;* Flatt & Scruggs: *The Versa-
           tile Flatt and Scruggs*).
           "The Knoxville Girl" (The Louvin Brothers: *Tragic
           Songs of Life*).
           There is even a double suicide in "Katy Dear" (The
           Louvin Brothers: *Tragic Songs of Life;* Ian and
           Sylvia: *Four Strong Winds*)—and the variant "Sil-
           ver Dagger" (*Joan Baez,* vol. 1).

    34   Modal singing done in true Appalachian style can
           be a little harsh on the ears at first hearing (listen
           to "The House Carpenter" on *Ballads and Break-
           downs from the Southern Mountains*). Less rough-
           hewn examples include "Shady Grove" on *Old
           Time Music at Clarence Ashley's,* vol. 2 and Doc
           Watson: *Good Deal;* and "Lady Margaret" on Ram-
           sey and Ray: *White Lightnin'—Fresh Air.*

    38   Several blues romance lyrics can be heard on Mis-
           sissippi John Hurt: *Today,* including "Candy Man,"
           "I'm Satisfied," and "Corrinna, Corrinna."
           "Frankie" (*Anthology of American Folk Music,* vol.
           1) and a variant, "Leaving Home" (*New Lost City
           Ramblers,* vol. 2).

    39   "Come All You Fair and Tender Maidens" (Mike
           Seeger); and a variant, "Little Sparrow" (*The
           Country Gentlemen*).

    41   A portrait of cowboys and their loneliness is de-
           picted in *Frontiers.*
           "My Love Is a Rider" (*The Badmen*).

    43   *The Essential Hank Williams* and *Honky Tonkin'*
           contain most of this important figure's best-known
           songs.

    44   "All the Good Times" (*Mountain Music—Bluegrass
           Style;* Flatt & Scruggs: *Folk Songs of Our Land*).

    45   For a variety of songs in this genre, see the Dis-
           cography for albums by Ray Price, Charlie Pride,

Porter Wagoner, and Marty Robbins, or listen to
any country and western radio station.

page 46   "He Loves Me All the Way" and "Stand By Your
Man" (Tammy Wynette: *Greatest Hits*, vols. 1
and 2).

48   "No Opener Needed" (Words and music by James
Talley. © 1973 by Rainmaker Music, Inc. All rights
reserved).

49   "That Girl Who Waits on Tables" (Ronnie Milsap:
Where My Heart Is).

Chapter 2

55   The album *African Music* shows the kinds of
rhythms and melodies found in traditional African
songs and dances. The transition of these styles to
the New World appears in *Negro Folk Music of
Africa and America*.

58   "Grizzly Bear" (*Negro Prison Work Songs*).

63   What has come to be known as "the blues," particularly with respect to chordal structure, first
acquired the name at the turn of this century. The
blues and many other contributions of black musicians are certainly a part of country music, but not
the "country and western" country music which is
the subject of this book. Accordingly, further discussion of black music will be confined to those
elements which entered or directly touched country
and western.

65   "Talkin' Hard Luck" (*New Lost City Ramblers;*
vol. 3). If this book had a filmography, the film *The
Grapes of Wrath* would be cited to show the plight
of Depression farmers. No wonder Woody Guthrie
chose Tom Joad as the subject for one of his ballads.

66   The New Lost City Ramblers: *Songs From the
Depression* gives a musical picture of ageless woes
of farmers.

page 69   "John Henry" (Sam and Kirk McGee: *Opry Old Timers;* Woody Guthrie: *Sings Folk Songs; Memphis Slim and the Real Honky Tonk; Richard Dyer-Bennett*).

70   "Nine Pound Hammer" (*Mountain Music—Bluegrass Style;* Flatt & Scruggs: *Folk Songs of Our Land*).
"Take This Hammer" (Flatt & Scruggs: *At Carnegie Hall*).

71   "The Wreck of the Old 97" (Flatt & Scruggs: *Folk Songs of Our Land*).
"George Alley's FF&V" (Flatt & Scruggs: *Folk Songs of Our Land*); or variant "Engine 143" (*Anthology of American Folk Music*).

72   "Talking Casey" (Mississippi John Hurt: *Today*).

73   "K.C. Moan" (*Anthology of American Folk Music,* vol. 3; Jim Kweskin: *Jug Band Music*).
"Railroad Blues" (*New Lost City Ramblers,* vol. 3).
"Folsom Prison Blues" (Johnny Cash: *At Folsom Prison*).

74   "Bringing In the Georgia Mail" (Monroe Brothers: *Early Bluegrass;* Flatt & Scruggs: *Hear the Whistle Blow*).

75   "Orange Blossom Special" (Flatt & Scruggs: *Hear The Whistle Blow;* Ramsey and Ray; *White Lightning—Fresh Air;* Johnny Cash: *At Folsom Prison*).

77   This story is quoted from HARD TIMES by Studs Terkel, reprinted by permission of Pantheon Books.
"Dark as a Dungeon" (Merle Travis: *Folk Songs From the Hills*).

80   "Chisholm Trail" and "I Ride an Old Paint" (Cisco Houston: *Cowboy Ballads;* see also Notes to Chapter 1, p. 00).

82   One of the few authentic touches in Western movies was the saloon piano player who blithely plunked away at tunes like "Golden Slippers" and "There'll Be a Hot Time in the Old Town Tonight".

Anything lively and fresh from the East (or even sentimentally maudlin and resh from the East) was welcomed in the West, hose residents maintained such a mixed bag of songs—a precursor of Western swing's melange of elements.

page 82   Jimmie Rodgers (*Train Whistle Blues* and *Country Music Hall of Fame*).

84   "Detroit City" (Bobby Bare: *Detroit City and Other Hits*).

85   "Six Days on the Road" (*The Big Country*). See *also* Dave Dudley: *Songs About the Working Man*.

Chapter 3

94   "Brennan on the Moor" (The Clancy Brothers and Tommy Makem: *In Concert*).
"The Golden Vanity" (*Richard Dyer-Bennett*); and a variant, "Sinking In the Lowlands Sea" (New Lost City Ramblers: *Gone To the Country*).

96   "Rake and Rambling Boy" (*Joan Baez*); and a variant, "Rambling Boy" (*Harry and Jeanie West*).

97   "Louisville Burglar" (*New Lost City Ramblers*, vol. 2).

98   "Wild Bill Jones" (*Mike Seeger*; Dock Boggs: *The Legendary Dock Boggs; Folk Banjo Styles*).
"Charlie Quantrell" (*The Badmen*).

100   "Jesse James" (*The Badmen; The Country Gentlemen*).

101   "Billy the Kid" (*The Badmen*).

102   "Texas Rangers" (*New Lost City Ramblers*, vol. 2; Ian and Sylvia: *Northern Journey*).
"Wabash Cannonball" (Roy Acuff: *Greatest Hits*; Flatt & Scruggs: *The Versatile Flatt and Scruggs*).

104   "Man of Constant Sorrow" (*Newport Folk Festival —1960*).
"King of the Road" (Roger Miller: *Golden Hits of Roger Miller*).

page 105 "Roving Gambler" (*Country Gentlemen;* The Everly Brothers: *End of An Era*).

106 "John Hardy" (*Folk Banjo Styles; Anthology of American Folk Music,* vol. 1; *Mike Seeger*).
"Stackolee: (*Anthology of American Folk Music,* vol. 1; *New Lost City Ramblers,* vol. 4; Paul Clayton: *British and American Murder Ballads*).

107 The quotation is from HARD TIMES by Studs Terkel, and is reprinted by permission of Pantheon Books.
"Darlin' Corey" (The Weavers: *At Carnegie Hall*).

109 "Long John" (*Negro Prison Work Camp Songs*).

110 "Foggy Mountain Top" ["If I had listened . . ."] (*Newport Folk Festival—1960*).

111 "Folsom Prison Blues" (Johnny Cash: *At Folsom Prison*).
Folk Banjo Styles contains examples of common banjo techniques.

113 *Anthology of American Folk Music* has examples of black guitar picking styles. Albums by Bill Monroe and Jim and Jesse feature outstanding mandolin playing, as do the Carter Family and the New Lost City Ramblers for the autoharp.
For Cajun music, listen to *Cajun Music—the Early '30's;* Doug Kershaw: *Spanish Moss;* and "Jolie Blonde" on Joan Baez: *One Day at A Time.*

114 For boogiewoogie and ragtime, listen to *Memphis Slim and the Real Honkytonk.*

115 For jug bands, listen to "K.C. Moan" on *Anthology of American Folk Music,* vol. 3; and Jim Kweskin: *Jug Band Music.*
Carter Family: *The Original and Great Carter Family* (also on *Anthology of American Folk Music*).
Merle Travis (*Folk Songs From the Hills*).

116 Dock Boggs (*The Legendary Dock Boggs*).

page 116   On the subject of interracial influences, see the article by John Cohen in *Sing Out* vol. 14, no. 6, January, 1964.

117   For Western swing, listen to Bob Wills: *The Best of Bob Wills and His Texas Playboys.*

119   *Early Rural String Bands* shows the progression toward bluegrass, as do the New Lost City Ramblers' renditions of string band music of the 1920's and 1930's.

The Monroe Brothers: *Early Bluegrass* shows the penultimate step in bluegrass music's development.

120   *Bill Monroe's Greatest Hits* contains songs which reflect the disparate elements which merged to form bluegrass: "In The Pines" (Negro blues), "Danny Boy" (urban popular sentimentality), and "Roanoke" (Appalachian fiddle breakdowns).

Country Music is something of a classic among bluegrass records (and, accordingly, most hard to find). For Scruggs's most recent involvement in inventive and contemporary banjo playing, listen to *I Saw The Light, Earl Scruggs: His Family and Friends;* and *The Scruggs Brothers* (where he accompanies his sons on a number of songs).

122   Other bluegrass performers to be found in the Discography include Jim and Jesse, the Osborne Brothers, the Country Gentlemen, Jimmy Martin, Roger Sprung, the Charles River Valley Boys, and the album *Mountain Music—Bluegrass Style.*

The quotation is from RUBY RED by William Price Fox.

124   "El Paso" (Marty Robbins: *Marty's Greatest Hits*). "Keys to the Highway" (*Meet the New Strangers*). "I'm Movin' On" (Hank Snow: *Award Winners*). "Handsome Molly" ["I wish I was in London"] (*Harry and Jeanie West; Country Music and Bluegrass at Newport—1963*).

125   "White Line Fever" (*The Flying Burrito Brothers*).

page 125 "I Wouldn't Live in New York City": (Buck Owens: *Wouldn't Live in New York City*).

126 "Homestead On The Farm" ["I wonder how the old folks . . ."] (Keith and Rooney: *Livin' On The Mountain; Country Music and Bluegrass at Newport—1963*).

Chapter 4

131 Very early Presley albums (especially those on the Sun label) are now almost impossible to locate, but his rural roots are evident on *Elvis Country*.

132 *Songs Our Daddy Taught Us* is another scarce-as-hen's-teeth album, but many of the songs are on the Everly Brothers' *End of An Era*. Its liner notes capture the spirit of the rock'n'roll decades. *Pass The Chicken and Listen* shows them involved in the "Nashville Sound."

"The Eighth of January" (*Folk Banjo Styles*). *The Weavers at Carnegie Hall* was recorded during the heyday of folk music's popularity, as witnessed by the audience's response. *Flatt and Scruggs at Carnegie Hall* shows the urban response to more countrified performances.

133 See the Discography for Newport Folk Festival albums and those recorded down South at the Galax and Union Grove fiddlers' conventions. Monroe: *Bean Blossom* was recorded at a bluegrass festival.

134 Ringo Starr: *Beaucoup of Blues*. For a transatlantic turnabout, Charles River Valley Boys' *Beatle Country* has the quartet's songs, bluegrass style.

135 Dylan joins Scruggs on "Nashville Skyline Rag" on Earl Scruggs: *His Family and Friends*. Listen also to Bob Dylan: *Nashville Skyline;* and Flatt and Scruggs: *Final Fling*.

page 135   *Joan Baez,* vol. 2 (with the Greenbriar Boys); *David's Album; One Day at a Time.*

The Byrds: *Dr. Byrds and Mr. Hyde; Sweetheart of the Rodeo.* Also *The Great Speckled Bird; Tim Hardin,* vol. 2; *The Band.*

Among many other groups into country rock are The New Riders of the Purple Sage (whose "Glendale Train" was obviously inspired by "Jesse James"); The Nitty Gritty Dirt Band, Canned Heat, Mother Earth, and Poco.

136   Ramsey and Ray: *White Lightnin'—Fresh Air.*

137   Several studio musicians have formed a group called Area Code 615. They play traditional and contemporary songs with a breathtakingly inventive and sophisticated manner.

139   Bluegrass 45 is the best-known Japanese string band in this country. Their *Early In The Morning* album shows a nice feeling for vocal and instrumental techniques.

140   Charlie Mingus: *Roots and Blues.*

The similarities between Dixieland and bluegrass are readily apparent to anyone who has heard both kinds of music.

142   "Tennessee" (Jimmy Martin: *Tennessee*).

"My Home's Across the Blue Ridge Mountains" (Joan Baez, on Earl Scruggs: *His Family and Friends*).

"To Get Back Home", words and music by James Talley. © 1973 by Rainmaker Music, Inc.

143   "Down South Blues" ["I'm going to the station"] (Dock Boggs: *The Legendary Dock Boggs*).

"W. Lee O'Daniel and The Light Crust Doughboys," words and music by James Tally. © 1973 by Rainmaker Music, Inc.

144   "Homestead on the Farm" (Keith and Rooney: *Livin' On The Mountain; Country Music and Bluegrass at Newport—1963*).

page 144 "Take Me Home, Country Roads" (John Denver: *Poems, Prayers, and Promises;* Loretta Lynn: *You're Lookin' at Country*).

145 "Take Me Back to the Sweet Sunny South" (*New Lost City Ramblers,* vol. 4; Joan Baez: *One Day at a Time*).

146 A recent example of this metaphor comes from Presidential candidate George McGovern's campaign characterized by the phrase "Come home, America" and the kind of popularism on which he based his campaign.

BIOGRAPHIES

Although this book has traced the development of country music in terms of its words and music, it would be incomplete to conclude without at least a few words about some of the more important performers, past and present, and some of the songs with which they are identified. By no means does the following roster include all of country music's landmark musicians, but it will help at least to introduce representative musicians of whom the reader should be aware.

ROY ACUFF: Closely associated with Grand Ole Opry, Acuff joined the radio program in 1940. He sings, fiddles (balancing the bow on his nose is a not unusual part of his act), and leads his band, The Smokey Mountain Boys. Some of the songs with which Acuff has delighted generations of fans are "The Great Speckled Bird," "Wabash Cannonball," and "Crash on the Highway."

EDDY ARNOLD: Few performers bridged the gap between country and "pop" music as successfully as did "The Tennessee Plowboy." Beginning in the 1940's, audiences all over the country enjoyed his "Bouquet of Roses," "Any Time," "Cattle Call," and "Eddy's Song" through recordings, as well as live and televised appearances.

CHET ATKINS: The variety of country music is nowhere better demonstrated than in this guitar virtuoso. His repertoire runs from traditional mountain tunes to Bach and the Beatles. Equally important to the industry are Atkins' innovations as a record producer which culminated in many elements of "the Nashville Sound."

GENE AUTRY: Discovered by Will Rogers, the "Singing Cowboy" starred in more than one hundred Western movies. His importance in country music comes from helping to identify it with the American West. Autry's hits have included "That Silver Haired Daddy of Mine," "Mexicali Rose," and "Rudolph the Red-Nosed Reindeer."

JOAN BAEZ: First achieving prominence at a Newport Folk Festival, Ms. Baez has gravitated from British ballads to contemporary country music. Her albums recorded in Nashville show a real feeling for country and western music.

GLEN CAMPBELL: Campbell has done much to make country music popular outside traditional circles through records and his television show. His best-known hits are "By the Time I Get to Phoenix," "Gentle On My Mind," "Wichita Lineman," and "Galveston."

THE CARTER FAMILY: A. P., Sara, and Maybelle Carter were among the very first rural musicians to be recorded. Their original songs and adaptations of mountain ballads, including "Homestead on the Farm," "Wildwood Flower," and "Keep on the Sunny Side," have endured over the past forty years, as have their techniques on guitar and autoharp.

JOHNNY CASH: Admired as much for his social involvement as for his singing, Cash reflects the way that country music can respond to contemporary influences. "Ring of Fire," "I Walk the Line," and "Folsom Prison Blues" are among his many successes. Cash's television show presented a wide range of musicians, including Bob Dylan. His wife, June Carter, of the Carter Family, performs with him on records and at personal appearances.

ROY CLARK: After years of radio, television, and live appearances, Clark achieved recognition as country music's "Man of the Year" in 1972 for his vocal and instrumental abilities. His hits include "Tips of My Fingers" and "Yesterday When I Was Young."

PATSY CLINE: Before her life was cut short by a plane crash

in 1963, Miss Cline achieved a number of successful records during her professional career: "Walkin' After Midnight," "I Fall To Pieces," "She's Got You," and "Faded Love."

FLOYD CRAMER: Cramer began his professional piano career accompanying many important country and pop artists, then going on to individual successes such as "Last Date" and "On the Rebound." His "slip-note" style of playing has become an identifying feature of contemporary country music.

JIMMIE DAVIS: Former Governor of Louisiana, Davis is best known for writing "You Are My Sunshine." His performance of gospel as well as secular songs has made him a favorite of older country music fans.

LESTER FLATT: An original member of Bill Monroe's band, Flatt left to team with Earl Scruggs and The Foggy Mountain Boys. Now appearing with "The Nashville Grass," Flatt's tenor voice and guitar accompaniment made him a hallmark figure in bluegrass music.

RED FOLEY: A featured artist on Grand Ole Opry, Foley had a succession of hits during the 1930's and 1940's, especially "Chattanooga Shoeshine Boy," "Just A Closer Walk With Thee," and "Peace in the Valley."

WOODY GUTHRIE: Although known as a folksinger, the legacy of Woody Guthrie was to make listeners more receptive to traditional rural lyric themes and melodies. Many of his compositions, including "This Land Is Your Land" and "Pretty Boy Floyd," continue to be performed by country and western artists.

MERLE HAGGARD: A leader in West Coast-based country music, Haggard's singing and songwriting reflects the basic elements of patriotism and family ties in rural music. His hits have included "Strangers," "Okie from Muskogee," and "The Fighting Side of Me."

KRIS KRISTOFFERSON: Renouncing academic and urban life for songwriting and performing, Kristofferson is among the most prolific of the "new breed" of country musicians. He is the author of "Me and Bobby McGee," "Help Me Make It Through the Night," and "Sunday Morning Coming Down" and other songs recorded by almost every current country artist.

LORETTA LYNN: A perennially popular female vocalist, Miss Lynn has had many successful songs, including "Don't Come Home a-Drinkin' " and "You Ain't Woman Enough."

UNCLE DAVE MACON: Uncle Dave was among the first headliners on Grand Ole Opry where his exuberant manner and banjo playing drew large audiences. His banjo techniques were to influence later generations of pickers.

ROGER MILLER: A "country-pop" entertainer, Miller writes and records a wide range of songs, including "Dang Me," "King of the Road," and "In the Summertime," all marked by his relaxed style and verbal inventiveness.

BILL MONROE: In the 1940's Monroe fused elements of traditional mountain balladry and Negro blues into bluegrass. Almost every important artist in that branch of country music has been a member of his Blue Grass Boys. Monroe's tenor voice and mandolin virtuosity have earned him the title of "Father of Bluegrass."

BUCK OWENS: A California-based singer and composer, Owens is well known for such hits as "Act Naturally," "I've Got A Tiger By The Tail," "Buckaroo," and "Your Tender Loving Care."

ELVIS PRESLEY: This country-bred performer became one of the world's most successful singers. From "Blue Moon of Kentucky" and "Heartbreak Hotel" to "Love Me Tender" and "Hound Dog," Presley drew on his rural antecedents to achieve unprecedented popularity in rhythm and blues and rock'n'roll.

RAY PRICE: A singer whose records consistently sell well, Price is best known for "Crazy Arms," "Release Me," "Same Old Me," and "Make the World Go Away." His singing against lush orchestrations and sophisticated arrangements was among the first in country music.

CHARLIE PRIDE: One of the very few Negroes to succeed in country and western music, Pride has enjoyed a number of hit records, including "Does My Ring Hurt Your Finger," "I Know One," and "So Afraid of Losing You."

JIM REEVES: Killed in a plane crash in 1964, Reeves's fame continues through his recorded performances of "Four Walls," "He'll Have to Go," and "When Worlds Collide."

JEAN RITCHIE: From a Kentucky mountain family, Miss Ritchie grew up amid a tradition of Appalachian balladry. She has performed at many folk festivals and night clubs and has recorded albums containing American versions of English, Irish, and Scottish songs.

TEX RITTER: A man whose singing reflected his roots in the Southwest, Ritter appeared in cowboy movies, and on records and radio shows. His hits include "Rock and Rye Rag," "Daddy's Last Letter," and "Hillbilly Heaven." Moviegoers remember his rendition of the title song of "High Noon."

MARTY ROBBINS: Both country and pop music can claim this singer whose successes include "That's All Right," "Singing the Blues," "A White Sport Coat," and "El Paso." His vocal style displays a strong feeling for songs which tell stories.

JIMMIE RODGERS: One of the indisputable landmark figures in country music, the "Singing Brakeman" sang, yodeled, and played the guitar in a combination of blues and mountain music, setting a standard for succeeding generations of artists.

EARL SCRUGGS: The name Scruggs has come to be associated with the five-string banjo. His innovative technique on that instrument set the tone for bluegrass music. He is now exploring new dimensions in both country and rock music.

HANK SNOW: Snow's recordings of "I'm Moving On," "I Don't Hurt Anymore," and "I've Been Everywhere" have insured him a highly regarded place in country music.

HANK THOMPSON: Inspired by Grand Ole Opry artists and Gene Autry, Thompson has achieved success with such songs as "Yesterday's Girl," "Waiting in the Lobby of Your Heart," and "Don't Take It Out on Me." He and his group, The Brazos Valley Boys, are country music mainstays.

MERLE TRAVIS: Guitar picker and songwriter, Travis is known for "Sixteen Tons" and "Dark As a Dungeon," as well as a syncopated instrumental technique he devised.

ERNEST TUBB: Star of radio and stage shows, Tubb recorded

"Walking the Floor Over You," "Have You Ever Been Lonely," and "Blue Christmas."

Doc WATSON: This blind guitarist from North Carolina reached national prominence for his phenomenal flat-picking. He has recorded albums with Flatt and Scruggs and the Ritchie family.

KITTY WELLS: Earning the title "Queen of Country Music," Miss Wells has had a procession of hits such as "It Wasn't God Who Made Honky-Tonk Angels," "Wrong Side of Town," "Heartbreak U.S.A.," and "Searchin' Soul."

HANK WILLIAMS: Ranking as one of the giants in the field, Williams was associated with scores of country classics, including "Your Cheatin' Heart," "Cold, Cold Heart," "Jambalaya," "I saw the Light," and "I'm So Lonesome I Could Cry." His own life reflected the agony of his lyrics.

BOB WILLS: An important fiddler and singer in Western swing music Wills led his Texas Playboys in "Rose of San Antone," "Mexicali Rose," and "Texas Playboy Rag."

TAMMY WYNETTE: Few female vocalists have had the impact of Miss Wynette, singer of "D-I-V-O-R-C-E," "Stand By Your Man," and "Your Good Girl's Gonna Go Bad."

BIBLIOGRAPHY

Books

BRAND, OSCAR. *The Ballad Mongers.* New York: Funk and Wagnalls, 1962. The rise of the modern folk song, and its commercial success.

COHEN, JOHN and MIKE SEEGER. *The New Lost City Rambler Song Book.* New York: Oak Publications, 1964. Lyrics and music to songs performed by the group, together wth excellent scholarship on the subject of "old-time" music.

CURRENT, RICHARD N. *et al. A History of the United States.* New York: Alfred A. Knopf, 1969. Useful for its discussion of the political, economic, and social development of America.

FOX, WILLIAM PRICE. *Ruby Red.* Philadelphia: J. B. Lippincott, 1971. A novel about the country music scene.

FRIEDMAN, ALBERT B. (ed.) *The Viking Book of Folk Ballads of the English-Speaking World.* New York: Viking Press, 1956. A collection of British ballads and other folk songs.

FURNAS, J. C. *The Americans: A Social History of the United States.* New York: G. P. Putnam's Sons, 1971. There is considerable material here on the culture of rural regions.

GILLETT, CHARLIE. *The Sound of the City.* New York: Dell, 1972. The rise of rock'n'roll, from its origins in hillbilly music and the blues.

HEMPHILL, PAUL. *The Nashville Sound.* New York: Simon and Schuster, 1970. "On-location" profiles of contemporary country and western figures.

HITCHCOCK, H. WILEY. *Music of the United States: A Historical Introduction.* Englewood Cliffs, N. J.: Prentice-Hall, 1969. A survey of the cultivated and vernacular traditions.

LOMAX, ALAN. *The Folk Songs of North America in the English Language.* Garden City: Doubleday, 1960. Lyrics and music to more than 300 folk songs, most of which fit into the country/rural category, preceded by fascinating introductions.

MALONE, BILL C. *Country Music U.S.A.* Austin: University of Texas Press, 1968. A comprehensive history beginning with the commercial era of country and western music.

OLIVER, PAUL. *The Meaning of the Blues.* New York: P. F. Collier, 1963. The relationship of the blues to the black experience.

RUSSELL, TONY. *Blacks, Whites, and Blues.* New York: Stein and Day, 1970. A study of black influences on white rural music.

SHELTON, ROBERT and BURT GOLDBLATT. *The Country Music Story.* New York: Bobbs-Merrill, 1966. A history in words and pictures.

STAMBLER, IRWIN and GRELUN LANDON. *Encyclopedia of Folk, Country, and Western Music.* New York: St. Martin's Press, 1969. Biographical entries of almost all of the musicians mentioned in the text and Discography.

TERKEL, STUDS. *Hard Times: An Oral History of the Great Depression.* New York: Pantheon, 1970.

WREN, CHRISTOPHER. *Winners Got Scars Too.* New York: Dial Press, 1971. A biography of Johnny Cash.

Periodicals

A trip to a library, newsstand, or folk instrument shop will reveal the variety of magazines and periodicals which deal with country music and related topics. They include:

Bluegrass Unlimited, Muleskinner News, and *Pickin'*—covering the bluegrass field.

Country Music—articles about the Nashville scene.

Old Time Music—published in England and containing scholarly articles about early rural American musicians.

Sing Out!—contemporary and traditional folk songs and news.

DISCOGRAPHY

The following list includes the titles of most albums mentioned in the text and the Notes, together with certain others; they offer a sample of the range of recorded country music. The Schwann Tape and Record Guide, particularly the supplementary catalogue, lists additional recordings by these and other artists.

Anyone who wants to approach early rural music in a systematic way can do no better than to obtain a Folkways Records catalogue and explore the music available on that label and the excellent notes included in each album. Library of Congress recordings also provide a fine selection of rural music, particularly early field recordings.

ACUFF, ROY. *Greatest Hits,* Columbia CS-1034.
African Music, Folkways FW-8852.
Anglo-American Ballads, Library of Congress L-7.
Anthology of American Folk Music: Vol. 1—Ballads; Vol. 2— Social Music; Vol. 3—Traditional Songs, Folkways FA-2951, -2952, -2953. A spectrum of authentic rural music—black, white, soloists, bands. A goldmine, with useful notes.
AREA CODE 615. *Area Code 615,* Polydor 24-4002.
————. *Trip in the Country,* Polydor 24-4025. Nashville studio musicians doing traditional and contemporary songs in inventive and virtuoso arrangements.
ARNOLD, EDDIE. *This Is Eddie Arnold,* RCA Victor VPS-6032.

ATKINS, CHET. Finger-Style Guitar, RCA Victor LSP-1383.

———. *Stringin' Along*, RCA Victor LSP-1236.

AUTRY, GENE. *Gene Autry's Greatest Hits*, Columbia CL-1575.

The Badmen, Columbia L2L-1011. Songs and anecdotes about legendary western outlaws.

BAEZ, JOAN. *David's Album*, Vanguard VSD-79308.

———. *Joan Baez*, Vanguard VSD-2077.

———. *Joan Baez*, vol. 2, Vanguard VSD-2097.

———. *One Day at a Time*, Vanguard VSD-79310.

Ballads and Breakdowns from the Southern Mountains, Prestige/International-25003. Appalachian singers and instrumentalists performing in centuries-old styles.

THE BAND. *The Band*, Capitol STAO-132. Rock-ragtime.

BARE, BOBBY. *The Best of Bobby Bare*, RCA Victor LSP-3479.

Bean Blossom, MCA 2-8002. Recorded at an important bluegrass festival, this album includes Bill Monroe, Lester Flatt, and Jim and Jesse McReynolds.

The Big Country, Mercury SRP 2-605. A mixed bag of modern country and western performers.

BOGGS, DOCK. *The Legendary Dock Boggs*, Verve Folkways FVS-9025. One of the earliest recorded banjo pickers.

BROWN, HYLO. *Sings Bluegrass*, Diplomat 2604.

THE BYRDS: *Dr. Byrds and Mr. Hyde*, Columbia 9755.

———. *Sweetheart of the Rodeo*, Columbia CS-9670. Two of the group's most countrified albums, infectiously done.

Cajun Music—The Early 20's, Arhoolie 5008. A collection of Louisiana bayou dance band music.

CAMPBELL, GLEN. *A Satisfied Man*, Pickwick SPC-3124. Campbell before he became country-popularized.

———. *Wichita Lineman*, Capitol ST-103.

THE CARTER FAMILY. *Original and Great Carter Family*, RCA Victor/Camden CAL-586. Re-pressings of their important recordings. Enduring landmarks.

CASH, JOHNNY. *At Folsom Prison*, Columbia CS-96. Songs of violence and recriminations performed before inmates.

CHARLES RIVER VALLEY BOYS. *Beatle Country*, Electra EK-74006. Liverpool, bluegrass style.

THE CLANCY BROTHERS and TOMMY MAKEM. *In Concert,* Columbia CS-9494. Irishmen zestily doing the sort of songs brought over by their settler ancestors.

CLAYTON, PAUL. *British and American Murder Ballads,* Washington WPL-727.

———. *Folk Ballads of the English-Speaking World,* Folkways, FA-2310.

CLINE, PATSY. *Great.* Vocalion 73872.

THE COUNTRY GENTLEMEN. *The Country Gentlemen,* Vanguard VSD-79331. Progressive bluegrass at its best.

Country Music and Bluegrass at Newport—1963, Vanguard VRS-9146. Some of the best pickers and singers.

Cowboy Songs, Ballads, and Cattle Calls from Texas, Library of Congress AAFS L-28 Authentic.

CRAMER, FLOYD. *This Is Floyd Cramer,* RCA Victor VPS-6031. The country pianist.

DENVER, JOHN. *Poems, Prayers, and Promises,* RCA Victor LSP-4499.

THE DILLARDS. *Live—Almost,* Elecktra EKS-7265. Infectious, amusing bluegrass.

DUDLEY, DAVE. *Songs About the Working Man,* Mercury MG-20899.

DYER-BENNETT, RICHARD. *Richard Dyer-Bennett,* Remington RPL-199-34.

DYLAN, BOB. *Nashville Skyline,* Columbia KCS-9825. One of the most important albums in country music discography.

Early Rural String Bands, RCA Victor/Vintage LPV-552.

THE EVERLY BROTHERS. *End of an Era,* Barnaby 2G-30260. Rock'n'rollers with a rural twang.

FLATT, LESTER and EARL SCRUGGS. *At Carnegie Hall,* Columbia CS-8845.

———. *Country Music,* Mercury MG-20358.

———. *Final Fling,* Columbia CS-9946.

———. *Folk Songs of Our Land,* Columbia CL-1830.

———. *Hear The Whistles Blow,* Columbia CS-9486.

———. *The Versatile Flatt and Scruggs,* Columbia CS-9154.

THE FLYING BURRITO BROTHERS. *The Flying Burrito Brothers,* A&M SP-4295. Country-rock.

Folk Banjo Styles, Elecktra EKL217.

Frontiers, Folkways FA-10003. Narrative with songs about the opening of the West.

Galax, Virginia Old Time Fiddlers' Convention, Folkways FA-2435.

GENTRY, BOBBIE. *Ode to Billy Joe,* Capitol ST-2830. Down home but modern.

THE GREAT SPECKLED BIRD. *The Great Speckled Bird,* Ampex A-10103. Ian and Sylvia go country.

GUTHRIE, WOODY. *Sings Folk Songs,* Folkways FA-2483. America's minstrel.

HAGGARD, MERLE. *Fighting Side of Me,* Capitol ST-451.

———. *Okie From Muskogee,* Capitol ST-384.

HAMMOND, JOHN. *Mirrors,* Vanguard VSD-79245. A young urban blues singer doing city and country blues.

HARDIN, TIM. *II,* Verve FTS-3022.

HOUSTON, CISCO. *Cowboy Ballads,* Folkways FA-2022.

HURT, MISSISSIPPI JOHN. *Today,* Vanguard VSD-79220. Delicate, charming blues guitar work and singing.

HUSKY, FERLIN. *Gone,* Capitol T-1383.

IAN AND SYLVIA. *Four Strong Winds,* Vanguard VSD-2149.

———. *Nashville,* Vanguard VSD-79284.

———. *Northern Journey,* Vanguard VRS-9154. *See also* The Great Speckled Bird.

IVES, BURL. *Greatest Hits,* Decca 7-4850.

KEITH, BILL, and JIM ROONEY, *Livin' on the Mountain,* Prestige/Folklore 14002. Good bluegrass.

KERSHAW, DOUG. *Spanish Moss,* Warner Bros. 1861. Contemporary Cajun songs and instructive album notes.

KRISTOFFERSON, KRIS. *Border Lord,* Monument KZ-3102.

———. *Me and Bobby McGee,* Monument Z-30817. One of the most successful of Nashville's "new breed."

KWESKIN, JIM. *Jug Band Music,* Vanguard VRS 9163.

THE LOUVIN BROTHERS. *Tragic Songs of Life,* Capitol T-769. Mournful mountain ballads.

THE LOVIN' SPOONFUL. *The Best of the Lovin' Spoonful,* vol. 2, Kuma Sutra KLPS-8046.

LYNN, LORETTA. *Coal Miner's Daughter,* Decca 75253.

———. *You're Lookin' at Country,* Decca DL-75310.

McGEE, SAM AND KIRK and the CROOK BROTHERS. *Opry Old Timers,* Starday SLP-182.

MACK, WARNER. *You Make Me Feel Like a Man,* Decca 75272.

MARTIN, JIMMY. *Tennessee,* Decca DL-4996.

MEMPHIS SLIM. *And the Real Honky Tonk,* Folkways FG-3535. Barrelhouse, boogiewoogie, and blues, with razzle-dazzle piano.

MILLER, ROGER. *Golden Hits of Roger Miller,* Smash 67073.

MILSAP, RONNIE. *Where My Heart Is,* RCA Victor APL 1-0338.

MINGUS, CHARLIE. *Blues and Roots,* Atlantic SD-1305. Rural-based instrumental jazz.

MONROE, BILL. *Bill Monroe's Uncle Pen,* Decca DL 7-5348.

———. *Greatest Hits,* Decca DL-75010.

THE MONROE BROTHERS. *Early Bluegrass Music,* RCA Victor/Camden CAL-774. Bill and Charlie play and harmonize.

Mountain Music—Bluegrass Style, Folkways FA-2318. An anthology of lesser-known bands, and a first-rate album.

Negro Folk Music of Africa and America, Folkways FE-4500.

Negro Prison Camp Work Songs, Folkways FA-4475.

Negro Prison Songs from the Mississippi State Penitentiary, Tradition TLP-1020.

THE NEW LOST CITY RAMBLERS. *Gone to the Country,* Folkways FA-2491.

———. *Songs from the Depression,* Folkways FH-5264.

———. *Vols. 1–5,* Folkways FA-2396, FA-2397, FA-2398, FA-2399, and FA-2395, respectively. With careful scholarship and great vocal and instrumental skills, this group has duplicated the sounds and spirit of early rural string bands and solo performers.

NEW RIDERS OF THE PURPLE SAGE. *New Riders of the Purple Sage,* Columbia C-30888. Another country-rock group.

THE NEW STRANGERS. *Meet the New Strangers,* Prestige/Folklore 14027.

Newport Folk Festival—1960. Vanguard VSD-2087.

NITTY GRITTY DIRT BAND and others. *Will the Circle Be Unbroken,* United Artists UAS-9801. A three-record set including Earl Scruggs, Roy Acuff, Merle Travis, and Mother Maybelle Carter.

Old Time Music at Clarence Ashley's, vols. 1 and 2, Folkways FA-2355 and FA-2359. A gathering of Appalachian singers and instrumentalists.

THE OSBORNE BROTHERS. *The Osborne Brothers,* Decca DL-75271.

OWENS, BUCK. *Best,* Capitol, ST-2105.

———. *Wouldn't Live in New York City,* Capitol ST-628.

POCO. *Picking Up the Pieces,* Epic BN-26460. Spirited country rock.

PRESLEY, ELVIS. *Elvis Country,* RCA Victor LSP-4460.

PRICE, RAY. *For the Good Times,* Columbia 30106.

———. *Greatest Hits,* Columbia CS-8866.

PRIDE, CHARLIE. *Best,* RCA Victor LSP-4223.

———. *Sensational,* RCA Victor LSP-4153.

RAMSEY, OBRAY, and BYARD RAY. *White Lightnin'—Fresh Air,* Polydor 24-4047. Two traditional rural musicians joined by Judy Collins and others. First-rate.

REA, DAVID. *Maverick Child,* Capitol SKAO-548. A talented singer-guitarist in a variety of country and country-inspired songs.

RENO, DON. *The Fastest Five-Strings Alive,* King KSD-1065. Good examples of Reno's distinctive banjo style.

RITCHIE, JEAN. *British Traditional Ballads in the Southern Mountains,* vol. 1, Folkways FA-2310.

RITTER, TEX. *Best,* Capitol DT-2595.

ROBBINS, MARTY. *Marty's Greatest Hits,* Columbia CS-8639.

RODGERS, JIMMIE. *Country Music Hall of Fame,* RCA Victor LPM-2531.

———. *Train Whistle Blues,* RCA Victor LPM-1640. One of the most influential country singers.

RONSTADT, LINDA, *Linda Ronstadt,* Capitol SMAS-635. Several country and western standards beautifully performed.

SCRUGGS, EARL. *His Family and Friends,* Columbia C-30584.

———. *I Saw the Light,* Columbia KC-31354. Scruggs is joined by people like Bob Dylan, Linda Ronstadt, and Joan Baez performing old and new songs.

SEEGER, MIKE. *Mike Seeger,* Vanguard VSD-79150. A New Lost City Rambler displaying extraordinary instrumental talent.

SMITH, SAMMI. *Help Me,* Mega 31-1000.

SNOW, HANK. *Award Winners,* RCA Victor LSP-4601.

SPRUNG, ROGER. *Plays Progressive Bluegrass,* Folkways FA-2472. From "Arkansas Traveller" to "Hello Dolly."

STARR, RINGO. *Beaucoup of Blues,* Apple SMAS-3368. The Beatles' drummer solo in Nashville.

THOMPSON, HANK. *Hank Thompson's Greatest Hits,* Capitol T-1955.

TRAVIS, MERLE. *Folk Songs from the Hills,* Capitol AD-50.

TUBB, ERNEST. *Greatest Hits,* vol. 2, Decca 75252.

Union Grove, North Carolina, 37th Old Time Fiddlers' Convention, Folkways FA-2434.

Versions and Variants of "Barbara Allen," Library of Congress L-54.

WAGONER, PORTER. *Country Feeling,* RCA Victor/Camden CAS-2321. A popular singer who's never lost his feeling for traditional singing.

WATSON, DOC. *Good Deal,* Vanguard VSD-79276. He's joined here by some of Nashville's best musicians—a knockout.

———. *Home Again,* Vanguard VSD-79239.

THE WEAVERS. *At Carnegie Hall,* Vanguard VRS-9010. The group that did so much to popularize folk music.

WELLS, KITTY. *Bouquet of Country Hits,* Decca 6-5164.

———. *Singing 'em Country,* Decca 75221.

WEST, HARRY and JEANIE WEST. *Harry and Jeanie West,* Archive of Folk Music FM-208. A nice feeling for mountain music.

WILLIAMS, HANK. *The Essential Hank Williams,* MGM S-4651.

———. *Honky Tonkin',* MGM E-3412. "Essential" is the word.

WILLS, BOB. *Best of Bob Wills and His Texas Playboys*. Columbia HL-7345. The original Western swingers.

WYNETTE, TAMMY. *Greatest Hits*, vols. 1 and 2, Epic BN-26486 and E-30733.

YOUNG, FARON. *Best*, Mercury 61267.

INDEX OF NAMES

INDEX OF SONG TITLES